THE MODERN WITCHCRAFT
Guide to
Magickal Herbs

Judy Ann Nock

YOUR COMPLETE GUIDE
TO THE HIDDEN POWERS
OF *Herbs*

Adams Media
New York London Toronto Sydney New Delhi

Adams Media

An Imprint of Simon & Schuster, Inc.

100 Technology Center Drive

Stoughton, MA 02072

First Adams Media hardcover edition December 2019

ADAMS MEDIA and colophon are trademarks of Simon & Schuster.

For information about special discounts for bulk purchases, please contact Simon & Schuster Special Sales at 1-866-506-1949 or business@simonandschuster.com.

The Simon & Schuster Speakers Bureau can bring authors to your live event. For more information or to book an event contact the Simon & Schuster Speakers Bureau at 1-866-248-3049 or visit our website at www.simonspeakers.com.

Interior design by Julia Jacintho
Herb illustrations by Claudia Wolf
Fauna illustrations in public domain via Wikimedia.org

Manufactured in the United States of America

10 2022

Library of Congress Cataloging-in-Publication Data
Names: Nock, Judy Ann, author.
Title: The modern witchcraft guide to magickal herbs / Judy Ann Nock.
Description: Avon, Massachusetts: Adams Media, 2019.
Series: Modern witchcraft.
Includes bibliographical references and index.
Identifiers: LCCN 2019035139 | ISBN 9781507211489 (hc) | ISBN 9781507211496 (ebook)
Subjects: LCSH: Witchcraft. | Herbs--Miscellanea. | Magic.
Classification: LCC BF1572.P43 N63 2019 | DDC 133.4/3--dc23
LC record available at https://lccn.loc.gov/2019035139

ISBN 978-1-5072-1148-9
ISBN 978-1-5072-1149-6 (ebook)

To all those who practice medicine and magick,

to all whose cures were revealed by their wounds.

And most of all to Jaime, my creative,

talented, beloved daughter.

Acknowledgments

Without the efforts of my agent, June Clark, and my editor, Eileen Mullan, this book would not have been possible. Without the meticulous input of Laura Daly, this book wouldn't be nearly as polished as it is. I would like to thank my beloved friend Leigh Ann Johnson, who not only provided me with focusing prompts; she also came to my side during the early stages of the manuscript and served as a research assistant as well as a vibrational healer. The Rev. Dr. Ann Gaba provided me with numerous resources that came from her vast experience not only as a consecrated priestess but also from her doctorate-level expertise in nutrition. Debby Schwartz, clairvoyant minister, priestess, witch, and true friend was a huge support and stood by me through many milestones. Barbara McGlamery propped me up when I felt like a wilted leaf. Stephanie Ritchie spoiled me and modeled exactly what unstoppable looks like. Jamie Roach was my champion and helped me believe this undertaking was within reach and encouraged me from start to finish. Dena Moes, intrepid traveler and award-winning author, shared in my triumphs and tribulations. My epicurean cousin, Darra Zankman, drew from her experience as a professional chef and sent me herbs and spices with which to experiment. Sumru Aricanli inspired me to pursue tasseomancy. I must also thank Donna Distefano, Sean Thomas, Julie Gillis, Amanda Sullivan, Johni Licht, Lily Miao, Christopher McCauley, Austin Nojaim, Faith Kimberling, and Louie Zhelesnik for real support and for showing up exactly when I needed you. That is everything. I thank the talented musicians of my band, Psych-O-Positive: Debby Schwartz, Louie

Zhelesnik, Andrew Gilchrist, and Karyn Kuhl for keeping it loud. I acknowledge and appreciate my Nock family, particularly James, Teri, Jackson, Jessica, Mary, Cynthia, John, Ben, and Samantha for doing the most important thing: supporting and sharing my work.

Throughout this endeavor, I was blessed with a powerful support network of truly magickal lightworkers. The creation of this book took everything I had. And decades before all those aforementioned beloveds who dwell so close to my heart stepped up and stood by me, a tiny seed was planted by Llisa Jones, who, in a certain way, introduced me to Susun Weed and set a story into motion. The first true instruction in herbalism I received was through Susun Weed. I grew up in Florida and enjoyed immersing myself in nature. One day in 1991, I was hanging out with a dear friend and Alexandrian witch, Llisa Jones, who showed me an advertisement for Susun's herbal intensives at the Wise Woman Center, located in upstate New York on Susun Weed's farm. The following year, I moved to New York City from the Florida panhandle, and my first independent excursion was to meet and learn from Susun. I found her to be a most generous soul, willing to barter with me and allowing me to stay in her house along with her apprentices, who were also there to learn the Wise Woman tradition. Susun taught us how to make simples and teas using oatstraw and nettles, how to forage for wildcrafted herbs, how to recognize edibles, and, most importantly, how to honor the earth, pay homage to the green goddess, and experience the intense link between herbs and magick.

I returned to the city, energized and inspired, and sought to continue my studies with one of Susun's protégés, an intensely intelligent woman named Robin Bennet. The New York–style workshop classes were starkly different from the immersive nature of the Wise Woman Center, and yet I was undeniably drawn to these knowledgeable, powerful women. I had the privilege of taking numerous classes whenever I had the opportunity and would continue seeking knowledge from wise teachers including Kathleen Gordineer at the New York Botanical Garden and the noted biochemical engineer Ursula Basch. Dr. Philip Barnett of The City College of New York, where I completed my master of science degree while working on this manuscript, helped me locate a wealth of research materials housed in the Marshak Library. And as before, I relied heavily on the institutions of the

New York Public Library and the New York Botanical Garden. Nicole Tarnowsky taught me how to access the specimens in the herbarium at the New York Botanical Garden, which was an incredible research experience. I write this not as some kind of herbal resume to justify my writing of this book but rather to acknowledge that I stand on the shoulders of giants, particularly women of power who were fearless in their pursuit and ownership of wisdom. I am but a delicate strand in a vast web, a tiny part of the sum of women's wisdom.

Nonetheless, thirty years as a practicing occultist has taught me a thing or two, and I recognize that my ability to share in this tradition is a true gift, a piece of magick in and of itself. It is interesting to note that the United States does not have a sanctioned herbal tradition. There are no officially recognized certifications, no governing body, nor state corruption of the herbal tradition of healing and magick that has spanned millennia. Every now and again, some government regulation will attempt to regulate and consequently stifle the wisdom and power of plants and witches' ability to use them. During these times, I quietly nod respect to the trailblazers who eschewed the medical industrial allopathic model of wellness and instead claimed, reclaimed, and disseminated the ancient wisdom of herbs. My immense gratitude extends to you all.

CONTENTS

Introduction

Plants are an embodiment of life and abundance on earth. We can learn so much from the myriad species of vegetation around us—resilience in the face of obstacles, the ability to continually renew and reinvent ourselves, and a desire to be of service to those around us. Within the enormous kingdom Plantae, herbs are particularly supportive companions to the modern witch. People have been harnessing the countless powers of herbs for sustenance, healing, and transformation for many centuries, even before the beginnings of witchcraft. Today, witches still turn to herbs to comfort and strengthen them on both a physical and spiritual plane. When using herbs and plants in magick, we do not view these entities as mere ingredients. They are our partners. They are living beings with awareness, reactions, and powers that they teach us and share with us. When a witch enters into a magickal partnership with herbs, healing and transformation take place.

In *The Modern Witchcraft Guide to Magickal Herbs*, you will explore this practical and potent knowledge of herbal applications and preparations as they relate to spells, potions, rituals, and more. Part I explains the history of herbal magick; the many ways to use herbs in magick, such as infusions, poultices, tonics, and sachets; and simple instructions for cultivating your own herb garden. Part II features profiles and illustrations of 100 common herbs so you can learn their characteristics and magickal properties. In Part III, you'll put all your knowledge to use via rituals and spells that use herbs to encourage good luck, divine your future, attract love, and much more. For example, you'll learn how to amplify your rituals by weaving an herbal crown of bay laurel, sage, and savory to wear during them. You'll concoct a love potion to encourage intimacy using orange blossoms and clary sage. You can protect your home by hanging a handcrafted herb broom made from mugwort and rosemary on your front door and see what's in store for you in matters of money and fortune by reading Moroccan tea leaves. You can even adorn your skin with a decoction of the ground-up leaves and seeds of the henna tree, then conduct a spell to invoke prosperity and health.

You'll also discover that this book is very hands-on: You will taste, smell, and understand herbs on many levels. Whether you are highly attuned with being a witch or are just getting in touch with the magickal part of yourself, you'll find wisdom in these pages. If you do not have experience working with herbs, you will find accessible step-by-step preparations to get you started on a lifetime path of discovery and practice. If you have been using herbs for years, you may learn a different ratio and proportion for scent, discover a new herbal tool, or come across a delicious recipe that can complement your thriving practice.

Herbal magick isn't just for individual use—these powerful plants also connect us to each other and to the past. It is comforting to know that the cycle of seed to leaf and flower to fruit will still hold sway and inform witches years from now, just as those who came before. As you discover and grow in this sacred path, know that the power of herbs has been here all along, ready to enchant, seduce, empower, inspire, and enlighten. Revel in the wisdom of ancient folk medicine that is still in use today.

Welcome to the magickal part of kingdom Plantae, where the mosses breathe and every blade of grass and the fruits of every tree sing the sweet heartsong of the great earth mother goddess. The conifers, the seedlings, the tender new leaves of spring, and the powerful dormancy of the sleeping trees—all these energies combine to vibrate the strands of the web of life. May you see this world anew. May this work harm none, and may it be of benefit to all beings. So mote it be.

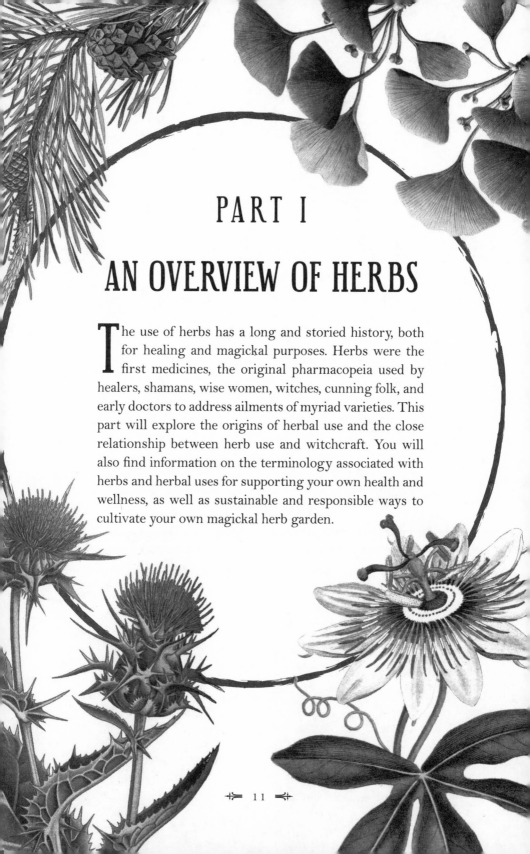

PART I
AN OVERVIEW OF HERBS

The use of herbs has a long and storied history, both for healing and magickal purposes. Herbs were the first medicines, the original pharmacopeia used by healers, shamans, wise women, witches, cunning folk, and early doctors to address ailments of myriad varieties. This part will explore the origins of herbal use and the close relationship between herb use and witchcraft. You will also find information on the terminology associated with herbs and herbal uses for supporting your own health and wellness, as well as sustainable and responsible ways to cultivate your own magickal herb garden.

Chapter 1

MAGICK AND MEDICINE: AN OVERVIEW OF MAGICKAL HERBS

There is nothing more humbling than the study of herbalism. With more than 15,000 different types of culinary, medicinal, and poisonous herbs, the list of their properties, uses, and effects is almost endless. Herbs are also undeniably connected to witchcraft—in fact, herbs are the embodiment of magickal essence. They are our living, breathing, working partners in magick. And they give up their lives for the benefit of all beings, to nourish, to heal, and to become an integral part of magick. Immediate lessons that we can take from herbs are to put down roots, turn toward the light, create what we need to survive, and to give back to those around us. We are in a symbiotic relationship with the denizens of flora upon the earth. In magick, we work together to bring about change.

HERBS AS SENTIENT PARTNERS IN MAGICK

Think of the life cycle of the plant. It begins as a seed, nestled in the dark, moist earth and then arises into the realm of air and sun only when conditions are right. An herb seeks nourishment by extending delicate hairlike roots down into the soil to extract water and minerals from the earth while simultaneously extending its energy upward, unfurling leaves to the sun, accepting light and changing it into food. This remarkable ability to transform the energy of light into sustenance connects the elements of earth, air, fire, and water.

As Above, So Below: Sacred Soil and the Root Connection

Plants are constantly reacting to their environment, particularly at the root level. In fact, a 2018 study published in the journal *PLOS One* showed that plants are able to communicate with each other through the vast networks of their roots. Unseen by human eyes, the plants and trees are busy recognizing their offspring and pushing nutrients toward them, sending out distress signals and issuing warnings when danger is near. Plants will create many different organic compounds through chemical reactions and secrete them through their roots. In this way, they are able to recognize each other as family or strangers and will respond accordingly.

Through analysis of the compounds produced in the roots of plants, the researchers who conducted this study were able to establish a connection between stimuli that plants would receive aboveground and the way they react to it belowground. This is a scientific affirmation of the magickal tenet "As it is above, so be it below." This tenet of witchcraft can be interpreted in many ways (perhaps most importantly to invoke the relationship between the witch and the divine mother goddess), but it can clearly apply to the power and communication abilities of plants and herbs as well.

What Is Hoodoo?

There is an entire magickal tradition that originated in Africa and is centered in the southern part of the United States called "root work." Also called "hoodoo," this tradition is also referred to as working roots, root doctoring, and conjure. Roots symbolize ancestry and the practitioner's connection to the land. To perform root work is to explore an intimate connection to the land, the herbs, and the ancestral line. Roots are actual and symbolic, representing the spirit world and the herbal world. Some examples of roots used in hoodoo are licorice root, calamus root, lovage root, and High John the Conqueror root. Other botanicals commonly used in root work include bayberry, borage, clove, and celery seed, among many others. Herbs and roots are incorporated into charms, sachets, and powders and are used to transform the energy of a person, place, or thing.

Sensitive Souls

Plants are highly sensitive to vibration and touch high above the ground as well. They react to the wind, to encounters with leaves from other plants, and to any sort of contact or touch. Canopies of trees will actually stop growing when they begin to encroach upon the presence of other trees. This practice indicates an awareness of themselves as individuals and of others in their community.

Anecdotal evidence has long held that plants respond to kind words and even music. Those believed to possess the "green thumb," a special talent for plant cultivation, were often known for speaking to their plants. Research now suggests that plants are even aware of when they are being eaten. Heidi Appel, PhD, professor of environmental studies at the University of Toledo, measured the responses of plants to different types of vibrations. In her quest to determine the awareness of plants, she re-created the acoustic patterns that a plant would encounter in the environment, such as wind, touch, or a caterpillar feeding on it. What she discovered was that not only could the plants distinguish between when they were being rustled by the wind or eaten; they would react by trying to defend themselves when necessary by secreting mustard oil, which caterpillars do not like.

Through the study of herbalism and its relation to magick, we seek to heighten our awareness of the relationship between a practitioner of magick and the herbs employed in spellcraft, rituals, and charms. We acknowledge the power of herbs and we honor them as potent teachers. Though it is impossible to master everything there is to know about herbs, we can still embrace this part of the natural world by putting the magickal bond between witches and herbs into practice. We can begin by learning how we define herbs.

WHAT IS AN HERB?

The most basic definition of an herb is a plant whose fragrance or taste lends itself to cooking, healing, or perfumes and colognes. An herb generally refers to the part of the plant that grows aboveground, mainly the leaves and flowers, but it can have alternate definitions depending on how the plant is both viewed and used. Herbs have many pleasing properties, including their taste, aroma, appearance, texture, and effects.

For most commercial purposes, an herb refers to plants used for culinary purposes. In this book, herbs will refer to either a plant or a specific part of the plant used for a specific purpose.

In the horticultural definition, an herb has a soft stem and does not have as much cellulose as other plants. Cellulose forms the rigid, outer wall of the plant cell. Herbaceous plants are most often used for their leaves and flowers and not so much for the seeds and roots (although all parts of a plant can be used for healing, culinary, and magickal purposes). Any nonwoody, vascular plant could meet the horticultural definition of an herb.

Herbs versus Spices

Also included under the umbrella term of herbs are spices, which are differentiated by their origin because they grow in a different temperate zone, the subtropical. When we think of spices, what most often comes to mind is the ground-up powder made from the dried seeds, bark, or roots of aromatic and savory plants.

Some other common terms you may encounter in your work with herbs include:

- **Annuals:** Plants or herbs with a growth cycle that lasts only one growing season. They germinate, grow to maturity, flower, and die within a year. As their name suggests, annuals need to be re-planted each year.
- **Binomial:** Each plant is identified by two names in Latin. The genus name appears first. This is the name that categorizes the characteristics that are shared with numerous plants. Following the genus is the species name. This name is specific and singular. It is never applied to any other plant. For example, the binomial name of basil is *Ocimum basilicum.*
- **Forage:** Foraging is the act of locating and harvesting wildcrafted herbs.
- **Hardiness zone:** These are eleven geographical regions of the United States that delineate climate conditions that affect the growing of herbs. Each adjacent zone is either approximately ten degrees warmer or cooler than the zone it touches.

- **Hydroponics:** A method of plant cultivation achieved without soil. Nutrients are dissolved into circulating water, and the plants are grown directly from the solution.
- **Organic:** The word "organic" refers to biological living matter, but in cultivation, it means that plants are raised without any additives such as pesticides or fertilizer.
- **Perennial herbs:** These are herbs that grow back year after year and do not need to be replanted.
- **Wildcrafted:** Wildcrafted herbs refer to herbs that grow in nature without human cultivation.

Before we move forward with your own cultivation and use of herbs, let's look back to honor herbalism's rich past.

A BRIEF HISTORY OF HERBALISM

Herbs were used by ancient people to address ailments and pain. Through trial and error, herbal remedies were created and passed down anecdotally through the generations. Monasteries were built around herb gardens to specifically cultivate herbs for their healing powers. These gardens became the first pharmacies and hospitals, where the sick would seek the healing powers of herbs. Meanwhile, wise women would cultivate other herb gardens and forage the hedgerows and woodlands, seeking remedies of their own.

An Early Monastic Mystic

Hildegard von Bingen was a theologian, musician, visionary, nun, and healer. She lived from 1098 until 1179. Among her published works were two medical volumes, *Physica* and *Causae et Curae*, which were inspired by her experience cultivating a monastic garden. Von Bingen's work was significant for many reasons: She drew connections between the health of the individual and the health of the surrounding environment; she detailed the many medicinal uses of plants; and she even included references to the four elements, the four directions, and the four seasons. Her books give us a fascinating glimpse into how herbs were used to treat illnesses in medieval times.

Herbs in the Ayurvedic Tradition

Ayurveda is possibly the oldest recorded medical system. Originating in India thousands of years ago, the literal translation of "Ayurveda" is "science of life." Ayurvedic medicine is a holistic practice, meaning that healing is focused on the entire being. This is very different from the Western tradition, which tends to focus on symptoms and treating them individually instead of looking at organisms as a whole. Ayurvedic medicine is highly personal and individualistic. Considered a traditional health system in India, Ayurveda incorporates treatments that may be derived from herbs, minerals, animals, and even metals. For example, turmeric is an herb used in Ayurvedic medicine to treat inflammation. Herbal extracts are administered along with diet and lifestyle interventions such as yoga.

Traditional Chinese Medicine

Dating back three thousand years, the use of herbs in traditional Chinese medicine, often referred to by the acronym TCM, is still widely practiced today. TCM incorporates a vast medicinal herbal component in its practice but also includes acupuncture, massage, exercise, and food to bring about therapeutic results. A holistic system, practitioners of TCM look for energetic interferences within the energy of the body. These imbalances are dealt with by looking at how the body is affected and the person is treated, not just the symptoms or the disease. The balance of yin and yang energies as well as a harmonious qi (or energetic life force of the body) is the goal of TCM. Herbs are used in preparations such as tonics, teas, tinctures, and encapsulated powders, and similar to Ayurveda, these herbs are combined with other treatments and lifestyle adjustments such as acupuncture and tai chi.

Western Herbalism: Dioscorides to Turner

The seminal herbal reference book by William Turner was published in England in three parts from 1551 to 1568. Turner was often called "the father of English botany," and his book, *A New Herball*, finally confirmed in writing information that had been previously passed down by word of mouth and sought to correct the many misnomers of the previously held quintessential ancient reference, the Dioscoridean herbal by Pedanius Dioscorides. Considered to be one of the most important scientific works of its time, Turner's book contained several illustrations, some detailed and others not, and some colored but not all. What is most important about Turner's *A New Herball* is that it sought to identify and describe the medicinal plants from the surrounding regions. Previously, healers and physicians depended on the Dioscoridean herbal, which described plants from the Mediterranean. Many herbs and remedies described therein were either misidentified or didn't exist at all, but were the result of the collective imaginings of people who wrote about things they had never observed. In the absence of empirical evidence, the misidentification of herbs resulted in the exacerbation of health problems rather than alleviating them. Turner sought to address this, and in so doing, created a tome that would inform on the future of herbalism.

John Gerard and the Generall Historie of Plantes

What began as a personal fascination that manifested as a garden influenced hundreds of years of herbalism. John Gerard's 1597 publication, *Generall Historie of Plantes*, detailed over one thousand species of herbs, many of which he cultivated and tended himself. Gerard's work that was heavily informed by the Flemish botanist Rembert Dodoens became known as the first botanical catalog. Not only did Gerard's herbal contain lists of herbs and plants, their habitats, and growing cycles; he also included their "virtues" or efficacies as well as the folkloric traditions surrounding their use.

John Gerard's publication followed Turner's by thirty years and provided readers with a much greater account of visual representations. And while Gerard acknowledged Turner for informing upon his work, Gerard included over 1,800 detailed engravings, which was a remarkable contrast to Turner's partially illustrated reference.

Nicholas Culpeper, the Radical and Champion of the Poor

No herbal history would be complete without referring to Nicholas Culpeper. Culpeper was a radical in his day but later came to be recognized as the first medical general practitioner. Culpeper treated the poor people of London, creating and prescribing herbal remedies for them during a time when diseases ran rampant and could decimate people. Culpeper often found himself at odds with both his contemporary physicians and apothecaries. His contributions are apparent in his publications *The English Physician* (1652) and *The Complete Herbal* (1653).

Because Culpeper translated Latin medical knowledge into English, he was among the first to make herbal remedies accessible to a greater population. *The English Physician* was the first medical book published in the United States.

A Trailblazer in Many Categories

Culpeper was also a trailblazer in the field of women's healthcare and was one of the first to recognize the role of women in conception. It was previously held that male semen alone was responsible for bringing forth human life and that women were the incubators of the seed. Culpeper suspected the egg's role and was considered radical for his revolutionary hypothesis.

Another interesting aspect of Culpeper's work was his widely known belief in astrology. Culpeper made strong associations between herbs and the planets and stars, which contributes to the magickal associations of herbs still held today.

The Greater and Lesser Planetary Correspondences to Herbs

Sun	Mars
• Mistletoe	• Garlic
• Angelica	• Onion
• Bay laurel	• Hops
• Chamomile	• Butcher's-broom
• Lovage	• Nettles
• Rue	• Horseradish
• Rosemary	• Wormwood
• Saffron	• Broom
• St. John's wort	• Tobacco
• Walnut	• Barberry
• Borage	• Hawthorn
• Marigold	• Hyssop

The Modern Witchcraft Guide to Magickal Herbs

Jupiter

- Dandelion
- Sage
- Betony
- Chervil
- Chicory
- Rose
- Endive
- Oak
- Chestnut
- Dock
- Sugar beet
- Fig

Saturn

- Oats
- Barley
- Rye
- Thistle
- Comfrey
- Elm
- Henbane
- Mullein
- Horsetail
- Hemlock
- Moss

Moon

- Chickweed
- Iris
- Cabbage
- Clary sage
- Willow
- Water lily
- Watercress

- Lettuce
- Poppy
- Cucumber

Venus

- Mint
- Violet
- Feverfew
- Mugwort
- Catnip
- Pennyroyal
- Thyme
- Tansy
- Burdock
- Marshmallow
- Vervain
- Plantain
- Lady's mantle
- Rose

Mercury

- Dill
- Clover
- Parsley
- Fennel
- Lavender
- Horehound
- Summer savory
- Valerian
- Marjoram
- Rue
- Caraway
- Oregano
- Clover
- Hazelnut

ANCIENT USES OF HERBS IN WITCHCRAFT

One of the most remarkably fascinating windows into the history of the magickal use of herbs is the Lacnunga (meaning "remedies"). Written in a combination of Latin and Old English, the Lacnunga dates from the tenth or eleventh century and contains a wealth of information on how herbalism was practiced with magickal intent. The author or authors of the Lacnunga also included methods for enchanting herbs with invocations and charms. This ancient pagan practice is the precursor to modern spellcasting, where words of power are combined with actions of intent in order to influence an outcome or event.

The Lacnunga also offers insight into how herbal medicine was practiced. Healing incorporated ritual, incantations, amulets, prayers, charms, and, of course, magick. One of the most significant entries is known as the "Nine Herbs Charm."

The Nine Herbs Charm

The Nine Herbs Charm is intended to promote healing and protect against illness and begins with an invocation. Translated by Bill Griffiths, the nine herbs are:

- Mugwort
- Plantain, referred to as "waybread"
- Lamb's cress
- Attorlape, believed to be either betony or cockspur grass
- Chamomile
- Wergulu, possibly nettle
- Chervil
- Fennel
- Crab apple

Before preparing any remedy with the herbs, a formal incantation is used to imbue the herbs with magick:

"THESE NINE STAND IN OPPOSITION AGAINST NINE POISONS.
RECALL {INVOKE THE NAME OF ONE SPECIFIC HERB FROM THE LIST
ABOVE}, WHAT YOU DECLARED,
WHAT YOU ESTABLISHED AT THE GREAT COUNCIL.
'UNIQUE' YOU ARE CALLED, MOST SENIOR OF HERBS.
YOU PREVAIL AGAINST THREE AND AGAINST THIRTY,

You prevail against poison and against infection,
You prevail against the harmful one that
travels throughout the land."

The Lacnunga instructs that a preparation may be made only after all the herbs have been spoken to. Each individual ingredient is to be ground into a powder as the aforementioned words of power are chanted or sung in repetition three times, creating a magickal charm. The powdered herbs are mixed with the juice of apples, water, and ashes, and then boiled with fennel and combined with egg in order to make a salve that can be applied to the body.

The importance of ritual magick combined with herbs is evident in the instructions because not only are the herbs sung to but the incantation is also sung to the person receiving the healing treatment. In fact, the incantation is supposed to be repeatedly sung into the mouth of the patient, into both ears, and also over their wound before the salve is applied.

The Land Ceremonies Charm

The Lacnunga also includes an elaborate pagan ritual known as "The Land Ceremonies Charm," which is intended as a blessing of the land to imbue it with prosperity, abundance, and fruitfulness. The Land Ceremonies Charm includes Christian symbolism but is undeniably pagan in nature. The Lacnunga outlines instructions on how to ritually and magickally prepare the land for cultivation. For example, practitioners are told to dig up four sods of earth from each of the four cardinal directions of the land that will be blessed. This task is to be undertaken at night before the dawn lights the sky. The incantation "Grow and multiply and fill the earth" is chanted over the sods as a potion made from oil, honey, yeast, milk, and herbs is then dripped three times onto each sod. The sods were then believed to be carried to a henge or stone circle or other sacred place and allowed to be touched by the first rays of sun as the new day began. Later, the sods were believed to be taken to church and left there until four masses were said over them by a priest. The holes from which the sods were removed were filled either with a cross emblazoned with the word "Grow" or, as hypothesized by Dr. Brian Bates, with rune stones. This act created a magickal circle that protected and blessed the field.

After replacing the sods, the next act of the practitioner was to face the east, the realm of new beginnings, and bow nine times while finishing with another incantation:

"WE ASK THAT THE SWELLING CROPS
BE WAKENED FOR OUR WORLDLY NEED
THAT THE FIELDED EARTH BE FILLED
AND THE GREEN FIELDS MADE BEAUTIFUL."

Finally, the practitioner would lie upon the ground in supplication after turning sunwise three times around and continue the invocative charm, asking the earth to become fertile and green so that the work may benefit the owner of the land and all who were subject to the owner of the land. Before any actual ploughing was done, the tools were consecrated as well. A paste made of frankincense, fennel, and salt was rubbed onto the plough while a seed was placed within it, all the while a charm invoked the power of earth:

"ERCE, ERCE, ERCE, MOTHER OF EARTH, MAY THE ALMIGHTY,
THE ETERNAL LORD GRANT YOU FIELDS GROWING AND THRIVING."

When the first trough of earth was turned over by the consecrated plough, a loaf of bread made with milk and holy water was placed within it, in a symbolic ritual of returning to the earth a portion of the blessed and desired yield. This act completed the elaborate ritual.

SECRET WITCH NAMES FOR HERBS

While some ancient rituals, like the Land Ceremonies Charm, contain Christian overtones, it was fairly common for herbs to be associated with witches. In *The Witch's Pharmacopoeia*, Peg Aloi (1999) describes many of the herbs that held secret witch names that were common in the Wiccan tradition:

Binomial Latin Name	Common Name	Witch Name
Erythronium americanum	Dogtooth violet	Adder's tongue
Bidens frondosa	Cockhold (also called devil's beggartick)	Beggar's tick
Glechoma hederacea	Alehoof	Ground ivy
Digitalis purpurea	Purple foxglove	Dead man's bells
Podophyllum peltatum	American mandrake (also called mayapple)	Duck's foot
Verbascum thapsus	Great mullein	Graveyard dust
Capsella bursa-pastoris	Shepherd's purse	Mother's heart
Euphorbia corollata	Flowering spurge (also called blooming spurge)	Snake milk
Chamaelirium luteum	False unicorn	Unicorn's horn

Secret names for herbs were necessary for two reasons: One, it protected the ingredients of the spell or charm, and two, it protected the witch. If no one knew or understood her spells and charms, a witch was less likely to be persecuted for enacting them. Using secret names for herbs was a method of self-preservation for early witches.

For modern witches, the use of secret names can be a way to pay homage to the past with the knowledge and respect that these secrets were necessary to keep the practitioner from harm.

THE BASICS OF HERBAL PREPARATIONS

Just as in antiquity, herbs today have many applications both magickal and mundane, culinary and medicinal. The main types of herbal preparations that we will be creating in this book are elixirs (something to drink) and topicals (something applied directly to the body). Let's look at the many ways herbs can be used for magickal purposes.

Infusions

Infusions are made by steeping a measured amount of fresh or dried herbs in a liquid such as water or oil. When using water, the water is heated to the boiling point and then either poured over the herbs or the herbs are submerged into the boiled water. The amount of steeping time depends on the desired effect:

- For a light beverage such as tea, an infusion can steep for as little as 5 minutes.
- For an oil infusion, the herbs are submerged into the carrier oil, covered tightly, and allowed to steep for 2–3 weeks.
- For a vinegar infusion, pour 1 cup apple cider vinegar over ¼ cup of your desired herbs and allow the herbs to steep for about a month, give or take a week depending on how much cellulose is in the plant material. Agitate the jar daily. Strain the liquid into a clean glass jar and compost the herbs when the steep cycle is complete.

Decoctions

Decoctions are necessary when the cellulose parts of a plant are being used. Rigid, woody leaves, stems, and roots will need to be decocted, which involves heating water to the boiling point, adding the measured amount of herbs, and then allowing the mixture to simmer while covered over very low heat for an extended amount of time.

It is important when creating a magickal decoction to allow yourself to enter into a meditative state and stay with your herbs. (This has a practical aspect as well, as you never want to leave a heat source unattended.) Decoctions are used for herbal roots, barks, and seeds or herbs that have a more rigid cell wall and require more time to break down. Remember that you can and should compost your herbs after removing them from the liquid.

Topicals

Topicals are herbal preparations applied directly to and absorbed through the skin such as salves, compresses, and poultices. Topicals can assist in the healing of inflammations, bruises, cuts, scrapes, and skin conditions. Topicals are commonly used to treat joint and muscle aches.

Compresses

A compress is made by soaking a clean cloth into an infusion or decoction and then applying it to the body in order to receive the healing benefits of the herbal preparation. Compresses can be either hot or cold and are commonly used to treat pain and swelling. To infuse your compress with magick, focus on the transference of energy and treat the cloth as a ritual object. You can imbue it with energy by placing it on your altar and exposing it to sunlight or moonlight depending on the type of effect you desire. Since a compress is reusable, think of the cloth as one of your magickal tools dedicated to the sacred task of healing.

Liniment

A liniment is made from an herbal extract that is then added to vinegar or alcohol. Liniments are used in topical applications for healing purposes. Liniments are good for treating strained and stiff muscles as well as bruises and sprains.

Tinctures

Tinctures are herbal concentrates made by soaking fresh or dried herbs usually in alcohol, but glycerin can also be used. The solution is kept airtight for 6 weeks, and then the liquid is strained off and the plant material discarded. Alcohol such as vodka is effective. Never use rubbing alcohol, for this is unfit for consumption. For those who cannot tolerate alcohol or wish to avoid it, glycerin is a good substitute, but the tincture can take longer to make. Glycerin is not as strong of an astringent as alcohol, but it still works. Tinctures are used to address internal issues such as digestion, fevers, or excessive mucus.

Poultices

Poultices are made by macerating fresh herbs in a mortar and pestle and then gathering them into a cloth and dipping them into hot or boiling water. Poultices are good for treating insect bites, skin inflammations, and cuts and scrapes.

The mortar and pestle is a magickal tool. It represents the sacred union of the goddess and the god. Preparing a poultice can be done as part of a ritual or spell. Use a mortar and pestle that is dedicated to healing. If you craft your own incense or use the mortar and pestle for other types of spells and charms, it is worth investing in a separate one that is devoted solely to healing and the use of tonic herbs.

Salves

Salves are topical ointments in which herbs, often in the form of essential oils, are infused into a beeswax and carrier oil base. Salves are used to heal wounds. A carrier oil such as jojoba, olive, or coconut is gently heated in a double boiler, and grated beeswax is added to add density to the carrier oil. A few drops of the essential oil are then diluted directly into the beeswax and carrier and gently stirred before the mixture cools. The result is an easy-to-apply topical that will last up to a year when stored in a cool, dark place where it will remain semisolid or in the refrigerator or freezer for an even longer shelf life. Cold-storing salves will harden them, however. They will need to sit at room temperature before applying.

Powders

Powders are made from the pulverized dried herbal material that can be used as filler for capsules in order to make them easy to ingest. Powders are commonly used in herbal supplements and are a typical way for small quantities of healing herbs to be taken for a specific ailment. For example, powdered valerian root is widely used as a sleep aid.

Simples

Simples, as their name implies, are herbal remedies that include only one herbal ingredient. Simples are easy-to-prepare elixirs and are generally drawn from the tonic herbs for the purpose of nourishing the body.

Teas

Tea refers to a specific plant, the *Camellia sinensis*. There are several common types of tea:

- Black tea is tea leaves that are fermented and dried.

- White tea is new tea leaves harvested before they fully open and are not fermented.
- Green tea is made from the mature leaves and buds that are not fermented.

The word "tea" is also used interchangeably for an herbal infusion or decoction. Tea can also refer to an herbal beverage, usually steeped for around 5 minutes.

Tonics

Tonics are liquid herbal preparations ingested for health purposes such as strengthening and healing. Tonics can be made from roots, leaves, berries, flowers, or bark of the desired herb and are either created by infusing or decocting and may contain a preservative such as brandy or another type of alcohol. A tonic is steeped for a much longer time than a tea, typically 20–30 minutes as opposed to 5, and a greater quantity of plant material is used. In the preparation of a tonic, you may use a cup or several cups of herbs, while in what most people think of as tea, only a few teaspoons of herbs are used.

Sachets

Sachets are made from dried herbs sewn into a small pouch for olfactory and magickal purposes. Sachets can be enhanced and their powers magnified by the addition of crystals, talismanic ingredients, or sigils. Sachets can be made from natural fabrics in any color that lends itself sympathetically for the spell at hand. For example, a money-drawing sachet could be made of green cloth, filled with sage and laurel, and sewn shut with gold thread.

Essential Oil

Used in a diluted state, essential oils are the volatile oil extracts of the leaves, stems, flowers, or other parts of a plant. Highly concentrated, essential oils are not used as topicals unless they are combined with a carrier oil such as jojoba, coconut, olive, or grapeseed. Essential oils should never be used as a topical in their concentrated state because they are volatile, meaning that they are easily absorbed and will damage skin tissue. They are only ever to be used topically as an active ingredient in a dilution.

Herbal-Infused Oil

An herbal-infused oil is made by covering fresh or dried herbs in a carrier oil and allowing the herbs to soak in the oil for weeks while stored in a dark and dry place (such as a cupboard) in order to create an extract. The herbal-infused oil will retain the scent and some properties of the herb used. After soaking for a minimum of 2 weeks and up to a month, the oil is strained through a cloth and stored in a dark covered container. Infused oils can be used for culinary purposes if tonic herbs are used. Infused oils can also be used magickally to anoint candles, clear crystals, and charge magickal tools. They can also be used to consecrate a person by anointing pulse points.

Oxymels

Herbal oxymels are elixirs of herbs combined with vinegar and honey. The honey acts as a sweetener that can make bitter herbs more palatable. For example, mullein is often used in oxymels to treat respiratory issues.

Not every herbal remedy is suitable to use in an oxymel. For example, carminative herbs used to aid digestion, particularly of fats, have to be bitter in order to stimulate bile production. To sweeten a carminative herb used for digestion would negate its carminative effects.

Percolation

A percolation uses gravity to extract the soluble components of an herb. A cone-shaped container or a closed funnel is packed with dried, powdered herbs that are moistened with the solvent until they are a "wet sand" consistency. Percolations are used to make tinctures, and although it is slightly more complicated than the infusion method, it is a much faster process. The herbs are covered with a mixture of alcohol and water and are allowed to steep, and the flow of liquid through the herbs is controlled. The percolation is collected in another container, and the spent herbs can be composted.

LOOKING AHEAD

From the history of Western herbalism to the different ways herbs are used, you now have a basic working foundation upon which to grow, and grow we must as we continue to explore our sacred connection to the earth, the land, the leaf, and the root through our magickal connection to herbs.

Chapter 2

SACRED SUSTAINABILITY AND CUNNING CULTIVATION

In order to sustain suitable mineral content, the earth must rest in between plantings. This chapter will sow the seeds on how to start growing your own herbs with magickal intent, taking into consideration climate, geographical location, and environmental sustainability. Planning and preparation can yield beautiful results. Choosing a site, providing appropriate substrate, and using magick in cultivation is a sacred endeavor.

The word "paradise" has its etymological roots in the Persian word for "garden." Creating an herb garden can bring you in touch with the earth and allow you to build a small paradise of your own design. Whether you have land to devote to cultivation or you are working in flowerpots, this chapter will delve into how to create magickal living herbal spirals, mandalas, labyrinths, and pentagrams to enhance the magickal power and appearance of your herbs.

THE EARTH: GIVER OF LIFE

The earth is a powerful entity, and our presence upon this planet is but one of many of her sacred stories. When we speak of protecting or healing the earth, what we really mean is that we desire to protect our own ability to live in harmony with the earth. By current scientific estimates based on the carbon dating of meteoric impacts, the earth has endured for approximately four and half billion years and will most likely continue to exist for another seven and half billion years until the sun fulfills its cycle of energy and absorbs all the near planets in the solar system.

Do Humans Impact the Earth?

The earth has withstood ice ages and tectonic shifts, and is now in a pattern of warming. Similar to humans, whose body temperatures elevate when a microscopic invader is present, it is not inconceivable that the changes in the earth's climate are due to our impact upon it.

The truth is, however, that the earth will outlast us. The earth is not in any danger. The danger lies in our own denial of the consequences of our actions and the fallacy that we will somehow be spared from the consequences by virtue of our rejection of their existence. If one ingests a poisonous herb believing it to be safe, one is not spared the consequence due to belief. If we wish to continue to receive the blessings and the bounty of the earth, if we truly wish to honor her and protect the diversity of flora and fauna that she shows forth, we must accept the gravity of our impact and understand what the earth needs in order to sustain us.

Giving Back to the Earth

In practicing magick, we invite the energy of the earth to inspire us, protect us, and heal us. Yet, we must also give back. We cannot only take. You cannot harvest if you do not plant. And you cannot grow healthy herbs if you do not nourish the earth. Even the food we eat has grown less nutritious over time. As the land is forced to continually produce without ever being replenished, valuable nutrients are stripped from the soil and they are not replaced; therefore, they are never absorbed by the plants. Since they were not present in the earth, they are not present in the roots, stems, flowers, leaves, and fruits, and, consequently, these essential minerals are not present within us either.

Humans have a symbiotic exchange of oxygen and carbon dioxide, just as plants do. By understanding that connection, we can see ourselves as linked beings. The witch and the herb are present with each other in the earth as well as the air. We are sharing this sacred space and working together. And we must do our part to give and not only take. Our magickal herbs deserve nutrient-rich soil in which to grow. We owe them that.

CREATION THROUGH COMPOST

One significant way we can give back to the earth is to compost some foods instead of throwing them in the trash. In some large cities, composting has reached municipal proportions. Keeping organic matter out of landfills is an example of good stewardship and sustainability. Decomposed organic plant matter can provide valuable nutrients to the soil that will nourish your herbs and also allow you to bring the cycle of life full circle. By observing how the summer grass dies and rises again, by being a mindful observer of the decay from which new life arises, we further our connection to the divine energy that creates these patterns, just as water, earth, air, and sunlight provide elemental magick as they flow through the life cycles of our beloved herbs.

Compost can be viewed as magickal. It is death and life. Sometimes referred to as "black gold," compost is the result of the decomposition of organic matter. It is a naturally occurring process that can be readily observed on a simple walk in the woods. You are likely to see fallen trees, a blanket of leaves, and annuals that have reached the end of their life cycle all in various stages of composting. In addition, mammals and insects digest matter, breaking it down and returning it to the earth where it becomes the bed for new life.

Composting at Home

To create your own compost, you will want to begin at Samhain, which is celebrated from October 31 to November 1. This is the witch's New Year, when the harvest is home and the fields have been reaped. There is also a practical reason for beginning a composting project near Samhain. It takes several months for organic material to break down into the prized soil enrichment. If you begin in mid- to late autumn, you will have compost by the spring, as this is ample time for microbes to break down organic substances.

Honoring the Goddess

It is customary to leave an offering to the crone goddess in your garden as a gesture of love and respect. As you cut the last of your herbs and bring them indoors to use or store, leave a gift of gratitude to the goddess of the waning year. Some examples of an appropriate gift would be the last apple of the harvest, a bundle of herbs, or a beautiful stone or crystal.

Compost can be made from matter such as fallen leaves, vegetable scraps, and the herbal material that is discarded after use, such as leaves, flowers, stems, and roots that have had their essence extracted through decoction or infusion. Avoid using any animal waste in your compost, as this can contaminate it in many ways. Bones and meat can attract rodents, marsupials, and other scavengers, and fecal material can contaminate the ground if not managed properly. In addition, dairy products take longer to break down and can delay the results as well as attract undesirable scavengers. While eggs are often considered dairy, eggshells are fine to use in compost, but it helps speed up the composting process if the eggshells are crushed before adding.

Choosing Your Site

Choose an outdoor location for your compost. You will want to choose a site that is not subject to runoff. For example, do not situate your compost under or near a rain spout. Too much moisture can create problems for biodegrading plant material into compost. Think of caring for your compost much in the same way as you care for your living herbs: Compost will need adequate drainage and exposure to the air.

Different Ways to Compost

Your compost can be a simple pile of material, or you can store it in a commercially built tumbler. You can also create a simple container with "chicken wire" affixed to 1" × 4" lengths of lumber with staples or nails that can be sunk into the site. The height will be determined by the volume you plan to compost. The type of structure that you choose should depend on how much compost volume you anticipate. For example, a large vegan family or extended community would benefit from a tumbler, as they have a larger capacity and are easy to turn. A smaller household or single person would not generate enough vegetative waste to warrant a commercial tumbler unless an abundance of yard clippings were involved.

Clearing and Consecrating Your Site

In composting, you have the opportunity to complete the sacred cycle of the seasons and honor the dead. The compost pile then becomes a magickal bed of transformation where energy extracted is returned to the earth so that new life may rise from it again when the time and conditions are right. After you have chosen your compost site, clear and consecrate the land. Rake or disrupt the surface, providing approximately 3 square feet for the compost. Kneel in a prostrate or prone position and place your hands on the earth. Close your eyes and project your energy into an alignment with the earth. All that is required for transformation lies beneath your hands. Set your intention of gratitude and replenishment, the acceptance of both the bounty of life and the death that follows. Whisper the following words:

"In darkness where the seeds have slept
The goddess with her secrets kept
Returns, returns, returns, returns
From death to life
From dark to light.
Subside and fall, return to earth
Await the spring for your rebirth
In perfect love and perfect trust
The earth holds all, the ash and dust.
From what has been grows what will be
By all the power of three times three
As I will, so must it be."

Structure and Layering Your Compost

As you begin your compost, you will need to make sure it can be aerated and agitated, otherwise it will not break down accordingly. That means it needs access to air, so it cannot be in an airtight container.

In addition, plan to distribute compost in layers with the following components:

- Brown material, which is external material that is gathered from the environment (leaves, branches, or twigs that should be chopped up before being added).
- Green material, which is internal material gathered from your home (vegetable scraps and vegetarian food waste). Even though it may seem counterintuitive, compost material such as coffee grounds and eggshells would qualify as part of the green layer.

The layers of your compost pile should alternate between brown material and green material. The brown material will emit carbon as it breaks down, while the green material will provide nitrogen. Both are essential to the process. Layering should be done in equal measure, and dry materials should be moistened with water before being added. Eggshells can be crushed to hasten the decomposition.

Letting the Composting Happen

Cover your compost with a tarp to keep it from drying out and observe the color changes as the organic material breaks down over time. Agitate it from time to time so that the contents get exposed to air. You can continue to add to it if you like, as the pile will gradually reduce. Fully composted organic material looks like rich dark earth. It is unmistakable. You will never doubt when it is ready to use. A properly managed compost will smell earthy, and it will be dank, but it will not have a rotting odor or attract pests.

What Is Vermicomposting?

Many people choose to use "vermicomposting," or worms, to break down their scraps. As the worms consume the vegetable scraps, they digest it and secrete it out as nutrient-rich humus, which can be added to your herb garden. The process takes approximately six months.

Depending on the volume, it can take a few months or even years for a compost pile to biodegrade. Be patient and know that you are reducing harmful methane emissions by keeping biodegradable material out of landfills while creating nourishment for your garden as well as participating in the cycle of life, death, and replenishment.

Indoor Composting

If you want to try small-scale composting indoors, you can place vegetable kitchen scraps in an indoor compost bin. Commercial indoor compost bins are readily available, or alternately, you can create your own. A plastic or wood container with a snug-fitting lid is a must. Additionally, there must be holes in the side for air circulation as well as holes in the bottom for drainage. The container must be situated on top of a tray so that any moisture will be caught and not spoil the surface upon which the compost container is resting. Line the bottom of the container with shredded newspaper and keep the compost moist but not sopping wet.

Here are some other tips for indoor composting:

• Well-managed compost will not produce an odor.

- It should be kept in a cool, dark place, such as underneath a kitchen sink.

Remember, be patient, and do not add meat or dairy to your compost. Fruit and vegetable scraps, herbs, teas, and even coffee grounds can be composted indoors.

Outsourcing Your Composting

If you'd rather not compost in your home or on your property, look in your local area for other options. For example, investigate if your local farmer's market will accept vegetable scraps for composting. Many will be happy to keep vegetable matter out of landfills.

CULTIVATING HEALTHY SOIL

The word "soil" is derived from the Latin "solum," which refers to earthy material. The main components of soil are quartz sand, air, water, and compost. In soil, we experience the potential for life that arises from death. In soil, we feel the conductivity of quartz crystal, worn down over time by wind and water. In soil, we feel the energy of life-giving waters as well as the presence of the very air we breathe. To touch the earth and to grow herbs is to interact with all elements: air, water, fire, and earth. It means paying attention to the environment and gaining intimate knowledge of herbs, your working partners in magick, and fulfilling their needs so that they may fulfill yours.

The Makeup of Good Soil

The composition of soil in your herb garden will vary depending on the needs of the herbs you intend to grow. As a general rule of thumb, you will want to include compost in your soil as well as some clay, silt, and quartz sand. Many herbs prefer soil that drains well because they originate from the Mediterranean region, so a good rule of thumb is to have your soil be composed of:

- No more than 15–20 percent compost
- Approximately 30–35 percent quartz sand (to provide drainage) and clay and silt (to hold moisture and nutrients)
- 50 percent that is automatically made up of air and water

While you can always buy commercially prepared garden soil, you will still want to add compost or other ingredients, such as vermiculite and perlite for structure so that the soil doesn't compress, or peat and clay to support soil health. These types of additives will benefit the specific herbs you intend to grow. For example, leafy flowering herbs such as basil and mint need phosphorous. Herbs that aren't getting what they need will tell you with their color and appearance. While some herbs do well in damp conditions, the majority require soil that drains well. Think flow: Nutrients need to be carried to the roots, absorbed, and replenished so the soil needs to be aerated and conducive to water flow, not compacted.

You will want your soil to start with a neutral pH, one that is neither too alkaline nor too acidic, and choose ingredients that will balance the pH depending on which herbs you intend to grow. For example, wood ash can make soil more alkaline by increasing the potassium level. Herbs such as parsley, turmeric, and chervil are high in potassium because they absorb it from the soil. If they don't get enough potassium, they will not grow abundantly and the leaves may appear curled or wrinkled at the edges.

DESIGNING A MAGICKAL HERB GARDEN

Creating and nurturing a magickal herb garden is one of the most transformative acts that a witch could ever do. It requires patience, commitment, attention, intention, wisdom, and knowledge both sacred and mundane. It doesn't matter how much space you have. Whether you are dealing with acres of land or small pots of earth, there is plenty of room for magick when establishing an herb garden. The deliberate intention of the sacred symbols incorporated into the design and the choice of herbs for ground cover, borders, height, and color, as well as their flowering cycle must all be considered carefully. In this section, you will find powerful suggestions for magickal herb garden designs that any witch would be proud to tend. The large-scale designs can be adapted for smaller spaces, and the potted designs can likewise be expanded to fill a larger plot of land. Whichever resonates with you is the one with which you will choose to work.

Selecting the Site

Survey the area you plan to use, evaluate the terrain, and allow yourself to visualize a sacred space. Speak to the ground on a spiritual level even as you take notice of its physical characteristics. Ask yourself the following questions:

- Is it relatively level? Planting on level ground will help you avoid erosion and runoff.
- Will your herbs enjoy full sun? Or, if there is shade, how many hours is the area in shadow? Leafy plants can tolerate shade, but you do not want to plan an herb garden where your plants will have to compete for resources.
- Are there other plants growing in the area? Not only can they interfere with sunlight; they will also compete for nutrients.
- Is the ground easy to till and care for?
- How much clearing needs to be done? Are there rocks, branches, and roots that need to be dealt with?
- Is there an ample water source nearby?

Considering these questions before you begin your magickal herbal garden design will help ensure the success of your endeavors.

The Three Sisters

Native Americans planted beans, corn, and squash together because these three plants have a beautiful relationship that the First People described as the "Three Sisters." These three plants were planted together and worked together to flourish. The corn's sturdy stalk provided the armature for the vines of the beans to grow, while the leaves of the squash plant gave protection from pilfering creatures. This type of companion planting brought nutrition as well as spiritual sustenance, as these three plants were grown together, honored together, and eaten together.

Preparing the Soil

When you have selected an appropriate site, you can add a layer of organic material on the top, either mulch or compost, and begin to till either with a spade, twist tiller, or rototiller if you prefer. Using a push or motorized tiller is useful if you need to turn over a large amount of sod or densely packed earth. You will want the roots of your herbs to have aeration and nutrients. If you turn a depth of 4–6 inches and mix in an organic layer, you will be off to a great start.

You can imbue this task with magick by reciting an incantation as you work:

> "THE SACRED EARTH
> THE CAULDRON OF REBIRTH
> BY WIND AND RAIN
> AN END TO PAIN
> TO RIGHT A WRONG
> A SEED GROWS STRONG
> WITH A KISS FROM THE SUN
> THE SPELL HAS BEGUN
> THE SACRED HERBS
> THE SACRED WORDS
> A THOUGHTFUL PLACE
> A SACRED SPACE
> IN WISDOM SOWN
> IN BEAUTY GROWN
> BY THE LAW OF THREE
> SO MUST IT BE."

Germinating Seeds

If you have plants that are already growing, simply plant them when it's appropriate for where you are. If you are working from seeds, however, you may want to germinate your herbs indoors where you can closely monitor them. Many herbs will do well when sprouted in peat pellets or small containers. You can transfer them after tertiary leaves begin to appear or when they have been growing for 4–6 weeks and all danger of frost is gone.

Keep in mind that transplanting is a difficult time for seedlings. They require tender care. Before their secondary and tertiary leaves appear, they get their nourishment from their primary leaves, the cotyledons, which will wither and fall off as the herbs grow. The cotyledon leaves are thicker and fatter than their regular leaves and provide the nutrients for the early stages of growth. This is why it can be appropriate to germinate indoors; your herbs are infants and are not ready to photosynthesize yet. When they start to get their regular leaves, they will be able to make their own nutrients from the sun.

As your seedlings begin to sprout, you can encourage them by telling them that they are magickal beings and that they are about to become a part of something wonderful: your modern witchcraft herb garden. Speak to them. Let them know your intent, that you have chosen them carefully and for a reason, that they will be your creative partners in aligning with the beauty of the land and the powerful earth energy that they effortlessly channel. Tell them you will sing together, breathe together, work together, and become one. You will enjoy days of sunshine and rain together and bear witness to the changes in each other. Your partnership has begun.

The Personal Herbal Labyrinth

You might want to consider growing a labyrinthian herb garden design, which can serve as an interactive meditative sanctuary. Creating an herbal labyrinth is a highly magickal endeavor that allows a witch to enter into deep communion with the land. Herbal labyrinths have a walking path of earth, mulch, or stone, and a border of herbs.

The Origins of Labyrinths

The labyrinth has its mythological origins in ancient Greece. King Minos, a demigod born from the union of Zeus and Europa, gave his name to the half-man, half-bull creature that was fathered by a white bull that arose from the sea. The minotaur lived at the center of the labyrinth on the isle of Crete and was overthrown by the hero Theseus with the aid of the goddess Athena. (Theseus would then become king of Athens.) Today, the labyrinth can serve as a powerful meditative tool. It represents a hero's journey into danger and uncertainty and emerging triumphant after receiving and accepting aid from the divine goddess.

An herbal labyrinth can be devoted to Gaia, Athena, Demeter, or any number of powerful deities held sacred in the Greek pantheon and still incorporated into sacred witchcraft today. Be sure to honor the spirits and gods from which the construct originates in order to avoid cultural appropriation. The herbal labyrinth is beautiful, and while it makes an appealing garden design, its true significance is sacred, for it rests in the relationship between deity and devotee, representing goddess energy intervening on behalf of those seeking to overcome obstacles.

Setting Up the Labyrinth

Creating a personal herbal labyrinth is best suited for an outdoor location with a growing plot of 12 feet or more. You will need ground that is relatively level and has adequate sun and good soil drainage as well as a variety of ground cover herbs, preferably edible varieties, so that they can be used in your magickal and culinary craft. Some suggestions are:

- Mint
- Oregano
- Red creeping thyme (*Thymus praecox "Coccineus"*)
- Sage (*Salvia officinalis*)
- Basil (*Ocimum basilicum*)
- Lemon balm (*Melissa officinalis*)

These aromatic and edible herbs are easily propagated by dividing established plants or by allowing cuttings to take root. Mint and oregano can be kept short by pinching off the tops. This will also encourage the herbs to bush out a bit while growing lower to the ground. Varieties of creeping thyme are fragrant, edible, and make excellent borders. If the creeping thyme grows too woody, you can always prune them, which will encourage the plants to rejuvenate. The other alternative is to harvest and then replace them.

These herbs do well in full sun and require soil with an alkaline pH that is well drained. To create the labyrinth, you will need:

- Mallet to drive the stakes
- 49 stakes
- Around 500 feet twine
- 24 small flags for marking
- About 150 feet rope to mark the walking path
- Wire cutters
- Around 30 feet of 18-gauge copper wire cut into 6-inch lengths and bent into a U shape to secure the rope to the ground
- Roundnose pliers
- Prefabricated border (optional)
- Mulch or stepping stones for the path (depending on your budget)
- Gravel, stones, or other border material
- Edging tools such as a hoe or tiller
- Compost

1. Choose your site and plan for around 12 square feet. Each part of this project is a meditation in and of itself. It will take planning, hard work, and patience. Clear the site and till the land, turning over the top layer of earth.

2. Use the following template to plan out your grid with twenty-four of the stakes and the twine. Each square of this grid represents 2 feet. Drive stakes into the ground with the mallet. Use twenty-four marking flags (or paper taped to stakes or even wooden paint sticks) to mark each box on the perimeter of the grid. Then, run the twine along the outer perimeter to create a large square. Secure the twine by tying, stapling, or taping it to the stakes. You can then run the twine vertically and horizontally to fill in the interior of the grid. You may want to use the remaining twenty-five stakes to indicate the interior coordinates, or you can write the coordinates on index cards and tape them in their corresponding place. Remember that the grid is only temporary so that you can create the path of the labyrinth and establish the planting areas in the areas adjacent to the rope.

A1	A2	A3	A4	A5	A6
B1	B2	B3	B4	B5	B6
C1	C2	C3	C4	C5	C6
D1	D2	D3	D4	D5	D6
E1	E2	E3	E4	E5	E6
F1	F2	F3	F4	F5	F6

3. Turn your attention to the center point. Stand in the center of the area that you intend to cultivate and get to know yourself anew in relationship to the earth. Stand with your feet shoulder-width apart and turn and face the east. Concentrate on the point where your feet touch the earth and remove your shoes if possible. Standing on the earth grounds you to the earth. Establish a root connection and allow yourself to feel the life within, beneath, and around you. This will be the center point of your labyrinth, the place to which you will travel in times of challenge. The center point will mark the halfway part of your journey and should represent a still point or a place of peace. Keep turning slowly until you have faced all four quadrants. As you turn, try to disrupt the surface of the earth a little bit so that you can visually observe your impact. This will also help you design your labyrinth, because this will indicate how wide the circumference of the center point should be, as well as the width of the path.

4. Take a moment to observe the center point that you have just indicated with your feet. This will be your destination on your spiritual path or meditative walk. Think about what you will place here. If you live in the Northeast, you may want to consider an apple tree. A citrus tree might be appropriate if you are in the South. If you are near water, a willow tree would make a meaningful center point, as would any sacred tree that is amenable to your geographical hardiness zone, such as oak, ash, hawthorn, or birch. Become familiar with your growing and planting zone so that you choose plants that will thrive. Other center points could be a water feature such as a scrying bowl on top of a pedestal or a birdbath. You may want to keep things simple and use a gazing ball to mark the center point of the labyrinth. Whichever option you choose, decide if you will want to sit in the center point, and leave space for this accordingly. After your labyrinth is constructed, you will want to be able to either walk around or sit and reflect at the center point, so be sure to make room for this.

5. Now that you have determined approximately how much space you will need for the center, you need to mark it. Using a length of twine, use the wire cutters to secure a piece that is half the length of your desired circumference to the center point. You can do this by tying one end of the twine to a stake and sinking it into

the center, then while holding the other end in your hand, tap the string to the earth as you walk around the center to mark the area. Use marking flags, small stakes, or sticks to indicate your measurements. You may find that your center point requires an area of anywhere from 2 to 4 feet, so the radius would be 1 to 2 feet.

6. Once you have established the center point, align yourself with the four directions: north, east, south, and west. Use copies of the blank grid to plan your path and the planting areas. Mark the center point with a stake as a reference point and remember to include the whole diameter of your center before you mark the labyrinth. Starting at the north point, you will mark a curve that begins like the top of a backward question mark and ends a few feet from the east point. Your next curve will be twice as long as the first one. Follow the pattern by laying lengths of rope on the ground beneath the grid. You can secure the rope using the cut copper wires. Bend them into a U shape with a pair of roundnose pliers and use the mallet to secure the rope so that each square of the grid resembles the plan. You will find that you may need to make adjustments as you go, and take a step back every now and then. (You can also look online for various labyrinth styles for ideas. Make as many copies as you need of the blank grid, and then transfer your plan to scale on your herb garden plot.)

7. Once the rope is secured, you can start creating the path. You can use a prefabricated border purchased from a garden supply store, mark the path with stepping stones, or with mulch. If you use stepping stones, you will not need a border; however, using a border will keep the mulch in place if you find that procuring stepping stones is cost-prohibitive. Use edging tools to make your borders neat. After the path is laid, take a moment to appreciate your work thus far. Walk the path and set your intention. It can be a place for contemplation, for focus, for de-stressing, for communing with nature, or whatever your soul requires. Once you have attuned with your path, the attunement will inform your planting.

8. Add a layer of compost to your planting area. Any place along the perimeters of the path will be suitable for planting herbs. You can use the lemon balm or mint as an herbal border along the path so that when you walk by and the leaves brush against your ankles, their scent will be released. Fill in all the negative space with the

herbs of your choice. You can use the ones suggested previously or choose others both for their virtues and appearance. Echinacea would be lovely in the harder-to-reach areas. With its tall purple blooms, it will provide a stunning visual element as well as a source of immune-boosting herb. It also will attract butterflies, as will day-lilies, bee balm, calendula, lavender, fennel, sage, nasturtium, and oregano. Choose herbs that will complement your work and enjoy tending your herbal labyrinth as it fills out and grows throughout the spring and summer. Take time to talk to the herbs and spend time in the center. May your work be of benefit to all beings.

RAISED BED HERB GARDENS

If your available space and resources do not permit the construction of a magickal design, you can opt for the more utilitarian raised bed herb garden, which can be every bit as beautiful and functional. Using raised beds allows you to control the substrate material and provides a barrier against erosion by wind and rain.

A raised bed can be almost any shape depending on your resources and inspiration. Most are rectangular, but you can also find round raised beds. Raised beds can also have multiple levels or trellises attached for climbing plants, which can add beauty as well as magick. You can affix magickal objects such as effigies of the goddess, ornaments, symbols such as spirals or pentagrams, or stones and crystals to trellises to augment their power and appearance.

You can also make a raised bed yourself with only the most basic of carpentry skills. A raised bed can even be built to be portable and can be small enough to fit on a porch, patio, or balcony. Herbs need a soil depth of approximately 4–5 inches, so your beds need not be very deep, but if you wish to create a portable herb garden, you will need a liner or plastic tub that fits inside the enclosing planter. Be sure to include drainage holes in the liner.

The Modern Witchcraft Guide to Magickal Herbs

CONTAINER HERB GARDENING

Container gardening has advantages in that herbs can be grown all year round. By choosing a container garden, you have the possibility of having all your herbs at stable temperatures, and they will never be blighted by an early frost. You are also liberated from the seasonal cycle. Although there is great benefit to attuning with the cycle of the seasons, if you wish to have a steady supply of fresh herbs all year round, then indoor container gardening might be the right cultivation method for you.

Choosing a Container

When choosing a container, a good rule to consider is that the pot or window bed needs to be at least as deep as the height of the foliage that the herb produces. This will give the roots of the herb an appropriate amount of space in which to develop. A 10-inch-diameter pot will be sufficient for a single herb. If you wish to include multiple herbs in a single pot, plan for a 20-inch-diameter pot, but be sure to put it on casters; otherwise, once it is planted and watered, it will be impossible to move due to its weight.

Setting Up the Pot

Containers should have a good potting mix. In addition to your own crafted soil mix of quartz, clay, and compost, you will also want to include vermiculite and perlite in order to make sure your soil does not become too compacted. Drainage saucers are imperative, and raising any type of container slightly off the ground is important for two reasons. First, it ensures airflow and evaporation of the runoff so that the delicate roots of the herbs are not constantly soaked, which can lead to rot. Additionally, it will give you a way to watch for water damage to the flooring if you are herb gardening indoors.

Adding Some Magick

Before adding soil to any container, you will want to place stones in the bottom of the container so that the drainage holes do not become clogged. This is also an opportunity to inject some magick into your container herb garden. Instead of using random rocks or stones, choose magickal stones with powerful sympathetic magickal energies. Even though they won't show, knowing that you have built your garden on a foundation of power will inform upon your relationship with your herbs. Using an array of tumbled stones such as carnelian, citrine, heliodor, aventurine, lapis, aquamarine, and amethyst will balance and attune the psychic energy signature of your garden. This transformative act will create the basis of your communication with your herbs. Remember that your herbs are your partners in magick, and they will absorb the intention under which they are planted.

Herbs That Grow Well Indoors

Choose herbs that will do well indoors. Some of the most popular herbs for gardening indoors are:

- Basil
- Chives
- Coriander
- Dill
- Oregano
- Parsley
- Rosemary
- Thyme

EMBRACE YOUR GREEN THUMB

Whether you have land to spare or a simple windowsill, you can create magickal herb gardens wherever you are. Expand your mind beyond the pervasive monoculture of lawns and think of the magickal life that surrounds you, life that you can direct, encourage, nurture, and sustain. This is the essence of modern witchcraft: creating meaningful change in unexpected places. Even a reclaimed dresser drawer could be the start of a little patch of magick! Now that you have a good understanding of what herbs need to grow and how to imbue your environment with magick, it's time to learn some edible uses for your magickally cultivated herbs.

Chapter 3

CULINARY HERBS: BASIC KITCHEN WITCHERY

The kitchen witch is a beloved magickal icon. While there are many different types of witches, those who practice solitary; with a coven; or in a specific tradition such as Gardnerian, Alexandrian, Dianic, Celtic, or eclectic, the kitchen witch is generally revered as a secular figure. Her altar is her home and hearth. Her coven is her community, and her spells and charms are edible and delicious. The kitchen witch stands less on formal ritual and ceremony; her magick lies in her everyday life.

The kitchen witch performs all tasks with magickal intent. Sweeping the kitchen floor is never just housecleaning with a kitchen witch. The cupboard broom becomes a magickal tool, and a routine chore becomes a banishing spell. Creating a meal is never just preparation and cooking. Her coven is her community, those who come to honor her table and take in the nourishment and healing that she provides. She is adept with culinary herbs and understands their magickal associations. She is just as likely to find her ingredients at the greengrocer's store or the farmer's market as opposed to an occult shop. In this chapter, you will gain a kitchen witch's understanding of the magickal properties of culinary herbs and how they can enhance spells. Learn which common culinary herbs are associated with astrology, goddesses, and moon phases as well as recipes with magickal herbal ingredients.

THE KITCHEN WITCH AND HER HERBS

Do you find yourself kneading intention into bread while you create the dough? Do you automatically stop to contemplate the chemical and physical transformations that occur when cooking? Do you feel a reverence for the beauty, aroma, and potency of the herbs you use? Do you find peace and power in a cup of tea, enjoying the transcendent state that most people associate with a meditation? If you answered yes to any of these questions, there is an excellent chance that you are a practicing kitchen witch.

The kitchen witch is often represented by a little doll on a broom. Originally from eastern Europe, the effigy of the kitchen witch is usually depicted in her crone form. With a prominent nose and chin, she sits upon her broom with either a kerchief or conical hat upon her head. Hung in a window, she brings good luck to the queen of the kitchen. Her energy is soothing, patient, and wise. She brings good fortune and wards against bad luck. She is the symbolic companion to the true kitchen witch, the one who rules the powers of fire, earth, and air to create magick and nourishment out of natural and pure ingredients.

Common Magickal Kitchen Herbs

Take a look inside your cupboard and do a magickal inventory. This will set you on the path of the kitchen witch; knowing which way to stir a pot to invoke or banish, and which herbs will serve your magickal intent in the best way. The most popular magickal culinary herbs include:

Binomial Name	Common Name	Parts Used	Magickal and Culinary Virtues
Pimenta dioica	Allspice	Dried berry, often crushed	Money drawing, prosperity, good luck; used in baking, particularly in cookies
Angelica archangelica	Angelica	Roots and stems	Purification, protection; used as a flavoring, particularly in candy
Ocimum basilicum	Basil	Leaves, fresh or dried	Peace, protection, happiness, love; used in pesto, sauce, soups, stews, salads, etc.

Laurus nobilis	Bay	Leaves, fresh or dried	Wisdom, divination, dream work; used to flavor soups and stews
Chamaemelum nobile	Chamomile	Flowers	Prosperity, peace, harmony, happiness; used as a tea to calm and settle the stomach; also used to induce sleep
Cinnamomum	Cinnamon	Bark	Success, spell amplifier, manifesting, energy, purification; used in baking
Syzygium aromaticum	Clove	Buds	Protection, purification, psychic ability; used in baking
Carum carvi	Caraway	Seeds	Protection, anti-theft, fidelity
Anethum graveolens	Dill	Seeds and feathery leaves	Lust, protection, good fortune; used in soups, stews, savory dishes
Allium sativum	Garlic	Root bulbs, fresh or dried and ground	Power, protection, healing; used in savory dishes
Zingiber officinale	Ginger	Root	Protection during childbirth, love, success; spell amplifier; used in teas, remedies, soups, stews, savory dishes
Origanum majorana	Marjoram	Leaves	Love, marriage, joy; used in similar ways as basil
Mentha	Mint	Leaves, fresh	Fertility, money drawing, success; used in salads and teas
Myristica fragrans	Nutmeg	Seeds, often dried and ground into powder	Psychic enhancement, happiness, love; used in baking
Petroselinum crispum	Parsley	Leaves, fresh or dried, also seeds	Offering to the dead, power, purification; used as a flavoring and as a garnish

Continued on Next Page

Binomial Name	Common Name	Parts Used	Magickal and Culinary Virtues
Rosmarinus officinalis	Rosemary	Needle leaves	Memory, wisdom, protection, healing; used as a flavor in meats, soups, stews, vegetables
Salvia officinalis	Sage	Leaves, fresh or dried	Purification, protection, clearing, wisdom, invocation; used to flavor meats, soups, stews, etc.
Verbena officinalis	Verbena	Leaves	Divination, inspiration

The Consecrated Cupboard Kitchen Witch Charm

When you are cooking with magickal herbs, your sacred altar will be your kitchen. You can mark this sacred space by creating a culinary-inspired herbal charm. For this you will need:

- 5 wooden spoons
- Hot glue gun
- 1 yard of ribbon in a favorite color
- 1 sprig fresh herbs that resonate with your work

1. Take the 5 wooden spoons and lay them one on top of another in a pentagram pattern. Using the hot glue, affix the spoons everywhere they touch.
2. Cut the ribbon in half. Use one portion to tie together a bundle of fresh herbs such as parsley, sage, rosemary, and thyme. Invert the bundle so that it is hanging upside down and tie it so that it hangs in the center of the pentagram.
3. Use the remaining length of ribbon to thread a loop through the top corner of the pentagram. Tie the two ends together so that your wooden spoon pentagram can hang on the wall, a cupboard, a handle, or over your stovetop to bless your kitchen. Use this incantation to give it a charge:

"Blessed be the hand
Blessed be the heat
Blessed be the sustenance
The nourishment we eat
Blessed be the gathering

The Modern Witchcraft Guide to Magickal Herbs

Blessed be the flame
Blessed be creation
Assembled in Her name."

You can include the name of a goddess or spirit energy at the end of the incantation to personalize your sacred kitchen.

INCORPORATING MAGICK INTO COOKING

Knowing which herbs to use and what their magickal properties are can change the way you cook. You can project an intention into your food and by using edible magickal herbs, and you will physically take in the energy of the spell or charm you wish to create.

Cooking with intention can also imbue your food with magick. Anything that you prepare with intention has the same power as a spell. For example, a ceremonial bread baked and eaten with magickal intent is every bit as powerful as a carved candle or a hand-sewn charm.

- Stirring a pot sunwise, or clockwise, is an invoking gesture; here is where you project those things you wish to call in or manifest.
- Stirring widdershins, or counterclockwise, will lend energy to those things you wish to release or ward off. Kitchen witchery can be a very intense and powerful type of spellwork because the crafting is done not only with intention but the results are taken into your body. Just as a freshly baked loaf of bread represents transformational elemental magick, so can herbs attune your psyche with the powers of water, earth, air, and fire. The fire element is not only the sun fire that allows herbs to photosynthesize; fire is also the hearth fire, the warmth of the oven and the stovetop, the brightly lit candles that grace the table when your beloveds gather.

EDIBLE FLOWERS

One way to create a magickal recipe is to use edible flowers. Flower eating has been a part of various cultures for centuries. Squash blossoms are frequently seen in Italian feasts, while in Japan, chrysanthemum tea is common. Roses and violets have been included in numerous dishes for hundreds of years. Modern witches can tap into the ancient practice of flower eating and add magickal energy.

Think of what the flower represents. In witchcraft, the goddess and the god are honored. The goddess manifests in her triple aspect: the maiden, the mother, and the crone. The flower is the maiden, the mother is the fruit, and the crone is the seed that is revealed at the end of the herb's life cycle. Adding flowers to your feast is a beautiful, magickal, and edible way to honor the goddess by having her represented as an integral ingredient.

Flower Maidens in Mythology

The Celtic goddess Blodeuwedd is one representation of the flower maiden. Another is Persephone, the daughter of Demeter. The goddess Flora, who was celebrated in ancient Rome, is another flower maiden who represents the season of spring.

Common Edible Flowers

Following is a list of edible flowers you can work into your cooking repertoire.

- **Borage blossoms:** The beautiful blue flowers of the borage herb have a light taste reminiscent of cucumber, and can be described as slightly sweet. Their sacred star-shaped petal formation makes them a magickal ingredient to salads. Because they are slightly sweet, you might enjoy creating sugared flowers with borage blossoms. (The directions follow this list.)
- **Chive blossoms:** Chives are a grassy herb with long, slender leaves that are richly aromatic. A part of the onion family, chives have beautiful lavender-colored blossoms with a flavor similar to chives, only milder. Add chive blossoms to any food in which you would use chives; for example, tossed in salad, sprinkled on an omelet, or even as a topping for potato salad or a garnish for cream cheese.
- **Dandelions:** The bitter-tasting leaves of the dandelion are a well-known remedy for aiding the digestion of fats, but the bright yellow flowers are edible too. Since the flowers also have a bitter taste, they make a lovely, if sharp, addition to salads. If you are

more interested in the aesthetic, try adding dandelion petals and honey to your favorite cornbread recipe.

- **Squash blossoms:** If you have ever grown any type of squash, you know how abundant they can be, especially summer squash. In order to avoid having an overabundance of zucchini, trim and collect the squash blossoms, which can then be used in a variety of ways, such as sautéing, frying, or used in a stuffing. Savory and delicate, squash blossoms have been a part of Italian cooking for centuries.
- **Calendula:** Although calendula is a type of marigold, do not confuse *Calendula officinalis* with tagetes, which are the marigolds commonly found in flower gardens. Calendula petals can be used in the same way as saffron—to impart color and flavor. You may want to dry and store calendula petals and use them for this purpose. Often referred to as "the poor man's saffron," *Calendula officinalis* can be used in starchy dishes such as rice, breads, and biscuits.
- **Nasturtium blossoms:** Nasturtiums occur in such a wide range of colors that they add a dramatic bit of magick to savory dishes. Their peppery flavor makes them an attractive ingredient to tossed salads or as a garnish for soups.

The Magick and History of Nasturtium

In 1596, Spanish physician and botanical collector Nicolás Monardes noted that each nasturtium petal had within it "a droppe of bloode, so redde and so firmely kindled in couller, that it cannot bee more." Monet featured nasturtium flowers in his garden, and Thomas Jefferson planted nasturtiums every year. Ancient Greeks likened the flowers and leaves to shields and helmets. This lends nasturtium to magickal energies such as protection, beauty, and vitality.

Summer Sugar Blossom Spell

The edible flowers just described can be crystallized with sugar and added to desserts such as ice cream, on top of cakes, pies, cupcakes, or almost any other sweet treat you are inclined to bake. Use them to bring your intention to fruition; to decorate a ritual feast; or to add sweetness, color, beauty, and joy to whatever sweet treat you may have in mind. By adding an intention to the process, you create a beautiful modern kitchen witch spell worthy of the flower maiden herself.

You will need:

- Selection of fresh, edible blossoms of your choice
- Small oak twig, sharpened to a point to make a stylus
- Parchment paper or wax paper
- Nontoxic marker
- Confectioners' sugar
- Empty, clean salt shaker
- 1 medium egg
- Small pastry brush
- Votive candle in a glass holder

1. Gently rinse the flowers and remove any stems. Carefully blot them with a paper towel to remove excess moisture. Allow them to air-dry.
2. As the blossoms dry, scribe the following numerical magick square of the sun on the parchment. Meditate and focus on your intention or desire until you can distill it to its essence and express it in a single word. Once the word is clear in your mind, use the key to find the corresponding number on the magick square with the letter of the alphabet. Write down the corresponding numbers to the letters in your key intention and trace the path of the numbers on the magick square to create a sigil. Put the magick square with the sigil to the side while you prepare the flowers, which should be dry by now.

MAGICK SQUARE OF THE SUN					
6	32	3	34	35	1
7	11	27	28	8	30
19	14	16	15	23	24
18	20	22	21	17	13
25	29	10	9	26	12
36	5	33	4	2	31

The Modern Witchcraft Guide to Magickal Herbs

Key:	I=9	R=18
A=1	J=10	S=19
B=2	K=11	T=20
C=3	L=12	U=21
D=4	M=13	V=22
E=5	N=14	W=23
F=6	O=15	X=24
G=7	P=16	Y=25
H=8	Q=17	Z=26

3. For example, to create a sigil for the invocation of love, you can lay the parchment over the grid and use a nontoxic marker to draw the sigil. Begin in space number 12 and draw a connecting line to 15. As you create these connections, you are thinking of your desired outcome; simultaneously creating a neural pathway in your mind. Next, you will continue the line from space 15 to 22, strengthening the pathway with your intention. Finish your drawing at space 5. You should have a drawing that resembles an incline or arc representing your journey from a starting point to the fulfillment of your wish. You can embellish your drawing with flowers and leaves to make your sigil beautiful. Remember that sigils can be as simple or as complex and specific as you need them to be.

4. Put about 1 tablespoon (or more, depending on how many blossoms you want to use) of the confectioners' sugar in the salt shaker. Separate the egg and discard the yolk. Beat the egg white until peaks begin to form. Dip the brush into the egg white and carefully paint the flower petals. Gently shake the sugar over the coated petals and allow any excess to fall off or gently blow it away. Repeat the sugar application. Allow the sugared flowers to dry completely on the parchment or wax paper.

5. As the flowers dry, envision the highest possible outcome of your intention transmuting from the paper into your flowers. The sigil informs upon the flowers as they dry. Allow the flowers to absorb your intention.

6. When the flowers are dry, fold the magick square and place it under the votive candle. Allow the candle to burn down as you enjoy your sugared flowers. Be sure to leave one flower out of

doors as an offering to nature and also remember to share one with a friend, especially if that person is in a position to impact the outcome of your intention. Take in the sweetness of nature and of life, made more potent by your intention and set into motion by your spell. Await the results with joyful anticipation.

ELIXIRS AND POTIONS

The classic image of the witch preparing a potion is iconic. Modern witches are more likely to craft a potion or elixir for enjoyment and wellness than to cast a spell on someone. Adding a pinch of magick can enhance your experience with food, as any kitchen witch worth her salt knows.

The following recipes are designed to soothe or stimulate, calm or excite, depending on your will and your wish. As you gather and bless your ingredients, you establish a soul connection. Eating and drinking is one of the most intimate things you can do. It engages all the mundane physical senses: sight, sound, taste, touch, and smell. Adding magick activates the metaphysical senses as well. When you take in nourishment, you are accepting strength and healing into your physical body, which can strengthen your psychic and magickal abilities as well. The body, the mind, and the spirit are intertwined.

We see this relationship of three entities in one form in many religions. In the Christian tradition, the trinity is represented by the father, the son, and the spirit. In Wicca, the trinity is embodied by the maiden, mother, and crone, and in secular witchcraft, the mind, body, and spirit complete the trinity. In witchcraft, the "law of three" is often referenced. What energy we send out is returned to us threefold. This serves as a karmic reminder to put forth good works into the world that may harm none and be of benefit to all beings. Creating magickal potions, elixirs, and feasts that are consumed in the body become part of the mind and spirit as well. Nourishment happens on many levels and at every level, magick is afoot.

Mystic Moon Milk

You can create a basic nondairy milk elixir and then infuse it with the herbs of your choice. Depending on your taste, Mystic Moon Milk can be enjoyed as a way to ground and center after a magickal endeavor such as a ritual or spell or as an offering or a libation. Typically, a portion of the libation is poured into the earth, signifying gratitude and honoring the earth. It is also symbolic of returning energy back to the earth and is a way to express thanks for blessings gained and insights received.

Consider your choice of seed or nut ahead of time: The seed represents potential and new beginnings, but its bounty is not revealed until the end of the cycle of flower and fruition. The nut is a culmination, the result of nurture and growth. Think about what your choice of ingredients represents and keep your intention focused on the outcome that you desire. You will need:

- 1 cup nuts or seeds of your choice (for example, almonds, pumpkin seeds, or flax seeds)
- Medium bowl
- 3 cups spring water
- Blender
- Strainer
- Cheesecloth
- Pitcher

1. To infuse your elixir with magickal energy, begin preparation on the night before the full moon. Pour the cup of nuts or seeds into the bowl and stir them gently, setting your intention. The direction that you stir will depend on your intentions. If you are creating magick in order to invoke something or bring something into your life, stir the seeds or nuts in a sunwise motion. If you are doing a spell to release something, such as an old pattern, stir widdershins. As you stir the seeds or nuts, envision the highest possible outcome taking place. Hold this thought in your mind as you recite the charm:

   > "From the tiny seed grows the mighty tree
   > And all that has been and all that will be
   > First will begin inside of me.
   > At the cycle's end, the fruit is revealed
   > Love is attained and pain is healed
   > At the sacred altar I have kneeled
   > My heart is warmed by the hearth's own flame
   > I speak my desire and give it a name
   > My heart is wild, free, and untame
   > That which I seek is seeking me
   > By all the power of three times three
   > As I will so mote it be."

2. Hold your hands over the bowl and project your energy into it. If you are using seeds, envision the cycle of life in its totality. If you are using nuts, envision the nurturing and growth that led them to fruition. When you have achieved this clarity, pour the water over the seeds or nuts and contemplate its power with a blessing:

"WATER OF LIFE

CRADLE OF EMOTIONS

THAT WHICH BRINGS FORTH CREATION

CLEANSING POWER AND PURIFICATION

ELEMENTAL POWER OF MYSTERY

I INVOKE YOUR GRACE IN THE NAME OF TRANSFORMATION.

MAY YOU PERMEATE AND MAKE WHAT WAS HARD PLIABLE

SO THAT THESE EVENTS WILL BEND TO MY WILL

AIDED BY YOUR POWER AND GRACE.

SO MOTE IT BE."

3. Allow the seeds or nuts to soak overnight, preferably near a window or even out of doors in the moonlight. As the moon waxes into its full cycle the next day, you are ready for the next step.
4. Pour the water along with the nuts or seeds into a blender and pulverize them together for a minute or until the mixture is smooth. Set the strainer over the pitcher and line it with cheesecloth. Slowly pour the mixture through the strainer into the pitcher. Gather up the cheesecloth and squeeze out any remaining liquid into the pitcher.

Now you can decide what to do with this elixir. You can refrigerate it (it will keep fresh for three days), or you can use it as a base on which to build more complex potions, depending on what energies you wish to align with. For example, instead of using spring water, you could soak the seeds in 3 cups herbal tea instead. Once you have created the Mystic Moon Milk base, you can add other ingredients by returning the base potion to the blender. Some variations you might want to consider:

Sacred Sun Milk

Use 1 cup sunflower seeds, 1 quart spring water, and a handful of dandelion blossoms. Allow the seeds and blossoms to steep in the sunshine. Let the mixture sit overnight. Strain off the flowers and pour the water and sunflower seeds into a blender. Add ¼ cup honey or agave to sweeten. Use as a base potion or as a powerful solar elixir in its own right.

Dram of Dreams

For a relaxing elixir to inspire your dreams, substitute an infusion of chamomile flowers for the spring water. Add 1 teaspoon vanilla extract and 3 tablespoons honey to the blender and run it again to mix. Warm up a cup on the stove and drink before dreaming.

Milk of Memory

To awaken past-life memories or to connect with the past and reawaken parts of yourself that you may have forgotten, substitute an infusion of rosemary for the spring water. Chop up a few dates and soak them overnight, then add them to the blender. Drink the potion before beginning a trance meditation.

Herbal-Infused Blessed Butter

Baking bread is a transformational part of kitchen witchery, and nothing goes better with fresh-baked bread than herbal-infused butter. Think of the butter as a permeation of pleasure. Creating a basic butter is easy and fun, and it only takes around 45 minutes, assuming the herbs have been soaked in oil the night before. Parsley and sage add flavor as well as magick. Sage is used for clearing and cleansing, and parsley represents gratitude, all of which are central to kitchen witchery. You will need:

- ¼ cup extra-virgin olive oil
- 16-ounce jar with lid
- 2 tablespoons finely chopped fresh sage
- 2 tablespoons finely chopped fresh parsley
- 1⅓ cups heavy cream
- Dash salt

1. Pour the extra-virgin olive oil into the jar. Add fresh sage and fresh parsley. Breathe in as you form your intention to smell the fragrance of the fresh herbs. Close the lid, allowing them to steep together overnight.
2. The next day, add the heavy cream and salt, so that the jar is about ¾ of the way full. Shake the jar vigorously for 30 minutes and check the consistency. The cream will begin to thicken, and eventually the fats will separate.
3. Strain off the by-product, which is buttermilk and can be used for other purposes, by pressing the butter against the sides of the

jar with a spatula. You can also strain it through a cheesecloth to remove excess moisture. Then you can transfer the fresh butter to another container or keep it in the same jar. Use it for your ritual breads, especially loaves that you bake yourself. When kept refrigerated, the butter will last 1–2 weeks.

FEASTING AND MERRIMENT

Sabbat rituals often conclude with feasting and merriment. Including magickal intention in your cooking is a wonderful way to prepare for the communal meal following a ritual. Even the preparation of food can be a ritual in and of itself. Adding auspicious herbs can amplify the magickal intent behind any sweet or savory dish. When you add herbs, you are not just adding flavor; you are adding a culmination of a seasonal cycle as well as the magickal properties associated with your herbs of choice. How you choose to do this will depend on the time of year as well as your intention.

Seasonal Connections of Common Herbs

Here are some magickal culinary herbs that will resonate with each season so that you know what to use and when:

Season	Herbs	Sabbats	Magickal Principles
Spring	Dandelion Mustard greens Red clover Nettles	Ostara and Beltane	Fertility and lust
Summer	Lemon balm Peppermint Spearmint Chamomile	Litha and Lughnasadh	Culmination and manifesting
Autumn	Parsley Sage Rosemary Thyme	Mabon and Samhain	Harvest and reaping
Winter	Cinnamon Clove Ginger Nutmeg	Yule and Imbolc	Repose and rest

Spring Blossom Magick Meal

For a spring ritual festival treat, try incorporating herbs and edible flowers into your feasting menu. Dandelions are abundant as they open their sunny blossoms in the early spring, making this activity a perfect kitchen witch recipe for Beltane and Ostara observances. (Wild foraged dandelions are the best. Avoid flowers from lawns or parks, as these are likely treated with pesticides, herbicides, and chemical fertilizers.) You will need:

- Approximately 40–50 wild fresh opened dandelion blossoms, free from pesticides, enough to fill a 2-cup measure when packed
- 1 cup breadcrumbs
- Small red onion, minced
- About 4 leaves fresh mustard greens, finely minced
- 2 sprigs fresh parsley with the stems removed and finely minced
- 1 medium egg
- 2 tablespoons Herbal-Infused Blessed Butter (see recipe in this chapter)
- 1 teaspoon horseradish
- 3 tablespoons tomato ketchup
- Salt and pepper to taste

1. Take all the dandelion blossoms and trim them so that all of the bitter greens are removed and only the yellow petals remain. Place all the loose petals in a large mixing bowl and add the breadcrumbs, minced onion, minced mustard greens, and parsley until all the ingredients are blended.
2. In a small bowl, beat the egg and then add it to the mixed herbs and breadcrumbs, tossing so that the mixture is coated in egg.
3. Take about ¼ of the mixture and roll it into a ball and then flatten it into a patty. Continue making patties with the rest of the mixture. Add the butter to a medium skillet and fry the patties on medium heat for about 4 minutes, and then turn once. Watch for a golden brown color to appear before turning.
4. Wash and dry the small bowl and combine the horseradish and tomato ketchup. Season with salt and pepper. Mix thoroughly using a fork. Use the mix to top the patties as a condiment. Enjoy a spicy spring herbal feast!

Summer Sorceress Salad

Summer brings the best salad greens. Not only are they highly nutritious, loaded with calcium and iron, fresh greens allow us to partake of the life force in the most intimate way. Consuming living greens connects us to the life cycle as we take in the energy of growth and incorporate it into our corporeal bodies. Adding a fresh green salad and homemade herbal dressing to your feasts is a magickal way to attune to the summer season. To make a summer salad worthy of a sorceress, you will need:

- 1 quart baby spinach
- 1 quart arugula
- 1 quart shredded romaine lettuce
- ½ cup herbed goat cheese, crumbled
- 1 tablespoon minced mustard greens
- 1 tablespoon minced fresh tarragon leaves
- 2 teaspoons wildflower honey
- 1 tablespoon apple cider vinegar
- Dash salt and pepper to taste
- ⅓ cup olive oil
- Torn mint leaves for garnish
- 1 cup borage flowers
- ½ cup orange nasturtiums

1. Wash the spinach, arugula, and romaine lettuce and allow them to dry by patting with a paper towel to absorb moisture or by spinning the water out. You can place all the washed greens in a colander with a lid and shake the water off.
2. Toss the spinach, arugula, and romaine together in a large bowl and sprinkle with the crumbled goat cheese.
3. In a small bowl, combine the mustard greens, tarragon, honey, and apple cider vinegar. Whisk the ingredients together, then add the salt and pepper. Keep whisking as you add the olive oil. Drizzle over the greens and lightly toss before blessing and serving. Top with torn mint leaves, borage flowers, and orange nasturtiums.

Autumn Olive Joy

A symbolic addition to your autumn observances, this edible mix is a combination of power and delight. The goddess Athena gave the gift of the olive tree to the people of Athens, winning her the dedication of the city. The Eleusinian Mysteries (rituals held in ancient Greece in honor of Demeter, the earth goddess) were celebrated at this time of year. You will need:

- 1 cup pitted black olives
- 1 cup green Spanish olives with pimento (peppers)
- 1 cup pitted kalamata olives
- 4 sprigs fresh thyme
- 4 sprigs fresh rosemary
- 1 large sprig fresh sage
- 1 large sprig parsley
- 3 dried and crushed bay laurel leaves
- 1–3 cloves garlic (to taste)
- Dash black pepper
- 3 cups extra-virgin olive oil

1. Drain all the olives and place in a large glass container with a lid.
2. Macerate all the herbs, including garlic, in a mortar and pestle to allow them to release their oils. Toss the macerated herbs with the olive mix. Sprinkle on the bay laurel and add a dash of black pepper. Pour the olive oil over the olives and cover.
3. Steep in the refrigerator for 2 weeks. After 2 weeks' time, remove the olives with a slotted spoon and transfer to a small bowl and enjoy! The remaining infused oil can be used for breads, dressings, or anointing.

Winter Secrets Biscuits

Winter is a time of dormancy for herbs. The silent, sleeping plant world achieves a state of repose. Indoors, we revel in warmth and keep the hearth fires lit. In kitchen witchery, this is an excellent time for magickal baking. These spicy round biscuits make an excellent repast for an addition to a winter full moon feast. You will need:

- 4 cups unbleached white flour
- 2 tablespoons sea salt
- 2 tablespoons baking powder

- 1 teaspoon ginger
- ½ cup butter
- 1½ cups Mystic Moon Milk (see recipe in this chapter)
- 2 teaspoons whole cloves

1. Preheat the oven to 450°F. Prepare a baking sheet lined with parchment paper. Combine all the dry ingredients together in a large bowl and mix them together thoroughly. Using a pastry cutter or two knives in opposite directions, cut in the butter until the mixture resembles small pebbles about the size of a pea.
2. Slowly pour in the milk and stir with a wooden spoon until the dough gathers and leaves the sides of the bowl.
3. Sprinkle some flour on a smooth surface and either roll out or pat the dough until it is around ½-inch thick or slightly less. Using a round biscuit cutter or a clean jar, begin cutting out rounds, then gather and roll the excess and cut again.
4. Line up a layer of rounds on the sheet lined with parchment paper. Place a single clove bud on the center of each round. Place another round on top so that the clove bud is hidden between the two rounds.
5. Place the pan in the refrigerator for half an hour, then bake for around 13 minutes or until the tops are golden.

From seasonal celebration dishes to sugary flower spells, herbs add aroma, flavor, and meaning to your rituals. Preparing and eating herbs is powerfully intimate; it is the ultimate transformation. Herbs also symbolize gratitude. The use of parsley as a garnish came from the practice of offering herbs out of respect for the lives given up in the name of sustenance. Using culinary herbs can be delightful to your palate, but the power of herbs transcends scent and flavor. Read on to learn about how herbs can be incorporated into your health and wellness routines for an even deeper connection to magick.

Chapter 4

WITCHES AND WELLNESS: INCORPORATING HERBS INTO YOUR SELF-CARE

Witches are healers, and herbs can be a central part of wellness and self-care. Before the introduction of pharmaceuticals, people would rely on cunning folk, ale wives, and wise women to attend to their health needs. Herbs were the basis of many healing preparations. The oldest-known description of herbs used for medicinal purposes dates back to the dawn of recorded history on an ancient Sumerian tablet upon which herbal remedies are inscribed. The herbs that were effectively used to balance the body, mind, and spirit in ancient times are still used today. This chapter will explore systems of health, different approaches to herbal healing, the application of archaic herbs in modern witchcraft, and herbal first aid.

HERBAL SYSTEMS OF HEALTH

Herbs have been used as an integral part of numerous systems of health for millennia across many cultures. Allopathy, naturopathy, homeopathy, and indigenous or tribal medicine are some common systems of health being used in the world today. Let's learn more about each one.

Allopathy

In Western society, the mainstream system of health is allopathy. The allopathic approach relies on reducing symptoms that a person or other organism exhibits, rather than on the being as a whole. Allopathy relies on the use of prescription drugs, which often contain phytochemicals derived from plants. In fact, 25 percent of prescription medicines are derived from plants. This is due to the presence of phytochemicals, "phyto" being the root of the word for "plant." Phytomedicines are synonymous with using the whole plant or herb. Phytochemicals are components of phytomedicines. The effective ingredients are isolated and used in a purified form in an allopathic system. The medicinal component refers to efficacy that has been demonstrated through clinical trials.

Some plant-based phytomedicines are sold in the United States as dietary supplements. Whenever you introduce an herbal supplement into your diet, it is important to remember that the word "natural" is not synonymous with "safe." It is possible to develop allergies even late in life, and any and all use of herbal preparations should be approached with moderation, caution, and respect for the power of herbs. It is your responsibility to investigate any side effects, countereffects, or possible allergic reactions, especially if you are already engaging in allopathic medicine.

Naturopathy

By contrast, naturopathy is a system of health that involves activating the body's ability to heal itself. The naturopath practitioner does not rely on reductionism to maintain health. A naturopath will look at an individual's needs and use natural remedies and various methods in order to aid the healing process. The healing process is viewed as an internal mechanism that can be amplified with specific remedies and regimens that are particular to the individual person. In addition to herbs and other natural products, a naturopath may also incorporate diet, exercise, massage, and detoxification into a healing process. In the United States, naturopathic physicians are required to complete a four-year graduate degree and pass licensing examinations.

Homeopathy

Homeopathy is a system of health that employs diluted ingredients that may be of animal, mineral, or plant derivation in order to address wellness issues by matching symptoms. The theoretical foundation of homeopathy is that "like cures like." A homeopathic remedy is meant to stimulate the body's natural healing process, which makes it similar to naturopathy.

Asclepius and Hygeia, Medical Deities

In mythology, the demigod Asclepius was born from the union of Apollo and the mortal princess Coronis. He became a hero as well as a god of medicine. His offspring were known as the Asclepiades. Among the Asclepiades was the goddess Hygeia. She was a companion of Aphrodite and is recognized as a goddess of health. Both deities incorporate the symbol of the snake into their representations, and together, they represent a balance of maintaining health and seeking cures. The snake is considered a magickal creature and also a symbol of health due to the fact that it renews itself through the shedding of its skin.

Homeopathy is different from naturopathy in that it is centered on symptoms, not the person as a whole being. The philosophy of homeopathy calls for very low doses of remedies, which makes the practice somewhat controversial. While it works for many people, it is difficult to ascertain exactly how the treatment works since the active matter is so diluted. It is possible that this is magick at its best: activating a body's natural ability to heal itself with the aid of diluted natural derivatives that cannot be explained by conventional scientific trials.

It is also interesting to note that while many people may present similar symptoms, different remedies may be prescribed by a homeopath. This also makes efficacy difficult to quantify by traditional scientific approval methods such as clinical trials. In the United States, homeopathic physicians are generally required to complete a four-year degree; however, licensing requirements differ from state to state. Homeopathic products are regulated by the Food and Drug Association, but there are no uniform standards for prescribing homeopathic remedies.

Indigenous or Tribal Medicine

Indigenous or tribal medicine employs magick along with herbs, animal, and mineral remedies. Tribal medicine is an oral tradition that is passed down from generation to generation, and one system may be entirely distinctive from other indigenous systems of health. The exclusive nature of tribal medicine lends it an air of magick, as natural remedies are accompanied with healing rites and rituals as well as cultural ceremonies that are centered on curing disease.

Tribal medicine is exclusive to the practicing members of a certain indigenous group of people, but it has had a huge impact on the world at large as awareness continues to spread. Consider the popularity of smudging, the sage-burning ritual used to cleanse and clear unwanted energetic entities in the surrounding environment, or the prevalence of sweat lodge ceremonies that are meant to link practitioners to their ancestors while simultaneously detoxifying their corporeal bodies.

Aromatherapy

Aromatherapy is widely used to treat a variety of ailments. In aromatherapy, medicinal-grade extracts from herbs and plants are diluted into carrier oils and then applied topically or taken internally. Aromatherapy, as its name implies, is also used to stimulate the olfactory senses.

Flower Essences

Flower essences were developed by Dr. Edward Bach in the 1930s. Bearing a similarity to homeopathy, flower essences contain trace amounts of plant material diluted in water and preserved with a small amount of alcohol. The philosophy behind flower essences is based on the idea that health is dependent on the emotional state of the individual. For example, in the Bach remedy system, gentian is used when you are feeling discouraged or depressed, while vervain is recommended for when you are high-strung. Oak is recommended for when you are overworked, and pine addresses feelings of guilt. The internal healing mechanism is activated by the stabilization of the emotional state and allowing illness to dissipate. Once the emotional state is brought into balance, then room for healing is made. Flower essences are also useful in magick, as they are by nature banishing potions that can either be taken internally or used topically.

What Is an Herbalist?

An herbalist is a person trained in the therapeutic administration of herbs. According to the American Herbalists Guild, an herbalist must complete 1,600 hours of study at a school of herbal medicine as well as 400 clinical hours. You will find that herbalists have a tendency to disagree with the isolated, allopathic approach to healing and wellness. Herbalists look toward the wisdom of nature and understand that nature provides a system of counterbalances. Using herbs in their complete form introduces an element of harmony to assist healing and wellness. The natural balance that is inherent in herbs can be experienced through the synergy of their complete form.

The Modern Witchcraft Guide to Magickal Herbs

AN HERBAL FIRST AID KIT

Herbs are ripe with therapeutic potential. Herbs have been used to stimulate healing in cells, tissues, and organs, and they can also be used preventively or as a treatment for an inflammation or illness. You may want to consider acquiring or growing a selection of herbs to have on hand for common problems that are bound to arise frequently. Sunburns, insect bites, upset stomachs, headaches, and even the stresses of daily life can all be effectively addressed with herbs.

Herbs can be categorized in many ways, but for the purpose of wellness, herbs used are labeled tonic, alterative, adaptogenic, or stimulating.

Tonic Herbs

Tonic herbs are generally safe and can be taken over long periods of time, such as six to nine months, with no ill effects. Some common tonic herbs include basil, rosemary, thyme, and mint. Tonic herbs are often used to balance or improve bodily functions such as respiration, digestion, reproduction, or endocrine activity.

Stimulating Herbs

Stimulating herbs have a stronger effect and are used for a much shorter duration. Stimulating herbs can be used to target a specific wellness issue such as an inflammation or other ailment. Stimulating herbs are powerful and should be used with care. Examples of stimulating herbs are echinacea and boneset.

Adaptogens

Adaptogens are stress reducers. They improve health by regulating and reducing fatigue, allowing the body to strengthen and heal. Tulsi (also known as holy basil), rhodiola, and ginseng are some examples of adaptogens.

Alteratives

Alterative herbs are taken preventively, as they build and enliven functions of the body. Some examples of alteratives are garlic, red clover, and red raspberry leaf. When you are feeling out of balance, using alterative herbs can bring you back to a state of well-being.

Growing a Healing Garden

You can cultivate your own healing garden the way cunning folk have done for centuries while bringing your modern sensibilities to your craft. Whether you wish to cultivate outdoors, in containers, raised beds, or on your windowsill, you may wish to consider this table of medicinal herbs that are common and easy to grow. Included in the table are the parts used and their effects:

Binomial Name	Common Name	Part of Plant Used	Effect of Use
Rudbeckia hirta	Black-eyed Susan	Juice of the root	Earaches
Salvia officinalis	Sage	Leaves	Astringent tonic, throat inflammations
Aquilegia canadensis	Wild columbine	Juice of the aerial part of the plant	Used as a topical for skin irritations
Monarda didyma	Bee balm	Tea made from leaves	Reduces nausea and vomiting
Mentha spicata	Spearmint	Diluted oil	Addresses stomach pain and nausea
Sinapis alba	White mustard	Seeds	Laxative effect
Melissa officinalis	Lemon balm	Leaves	Calming aroma and amplifies the effects of other herbs
Stachys byzantina	Lamb's ear	Root and leaves	Roots are used to induce vomiting (purgative), leaves can be used as finger bandages
Daucus carota	Queen Anne's lace	Leaves and seeds	Used to treat colic and flatulence (carminative)
Parthenium	Feverfew	Tonic made from leaves	Soothes headaches
Tanacetum vulgare	Tansy	Diluted oil	Insect repellant
Artemisia absinthium	Wormwood	Diluted oil	Digestive aid, stimulates gallbladder

Sanguisorba	Burnet	Leaf	Chewing on the leaves aids digestion while a tea can stop diarrhea
Saponaria officinalis	Soapwort	Root	Used to treat coughs, gout, jaundice, and rheumatism
Viola odorata	Violet	Leaves and flowers	Used as an emollient and a laxative
Alcea rosea	Hollyhock	Root	Emollient, diuretic, and demulcent
Iris foetidissima	Iris	Root	Wound cleansing, eaten after boiling, aids spleen and gallbladder
Asclepias tuberosa	Milkweed	Root, flowers	Used to treat lung ailments such as bronchitis

HERBAL OXYMELS

An oxymel is an elixir of herbs combined with vinegar and honey. Oxymels have been in existence since the time of classical Greek society, and they are enjoying a resurgence among modern herbalists and witches as a relatively easy way to create healthful potions. Oxymels are primarily used in wellness remedies to support respiratory function, and their uses are many. An oxymel will contain three basic ingredients: fresh or dried herbs, honey, and apple cider vinegar. The herbs, honey, and vinegar are inherently magickal:

- The sacred bee priestesses of Aphrodite were called the melissae.
- Inside of an apple, the pattern of seed arrangement is reminiscent of the pentagram.
- Herbs are perhaps our strongest tie to Gaia, the great earth mother.

Oxymels are pleasing to the taste, making them incredibly versatile. Oxymels can be taken by the spoonful, dissolved in water, or added to food such as salads or yogurt, even waffles and pancakes. How you choose to ingest your oxymel is up to your own personal taste. Creating an oxymel can be achieved in many different ways. You will need:

- ⅓ cup mullein, elecampane, echinacea, elderberry, or the immune-boosting herbs of your choice
- 2 clear pint glass jars, each with a lid

- ⅔ cup apple cider vinegar
- ¾ cup wildflower honey

1. Begin on the first quarter moon and bless your herbs with a modern charm such as:

"WIND AND RAIN

SUN AND WATER

THE WAXING LIGHT

THE DARK MOON'S DAUGHTER

GATHERED TOGETHER

FROM FIELD TO HEARTH

GATHERED TOGETHER

BORN OF THE EARTH

TO HAVE AND TO HEAL

TO REMEMBER AND FEEL

A RETURN TO HEALTH

THE ONLY TRUE WEALTH

THE SACRED HERB

THE SACRED WORD

BOUND IN DEED

FROM STEM TO SEED

INVOKE THE REMEDY

AND BANISH THE MALADY

BY ALL THE STRENGTH OF THREE TIMES THREE

AS I WILL SO MUST IT BE."

2. Place the herbs or herbal blend in the pint jar. Cover with the apple cider vinegar, then add the honey. Close the lid on the jar and shake to mix. Store the mixture in a cool, dark, and dry place. As the moon waxes, focus on the transference of energy from the herbs to the potion. Attune with your creation as you take the jar out every few days and shake it. Project your intention into the jar and enchant it with a charm:

"HONEY AND HERB,

CIDER—COMBINE!

MAY RADIANT HEALTH

ALWAYS BE MINE

HERB OF EARTH

APPLES OF LOVE

As it is below
So it is above
Honey from comb
These three are now one
As it is my will
So must it be done!"

3. Allow the herbs to steep for at least 2 weeks. At the end of 2 weeks' time, when the moon is full, strain the potion into another glass jar. It is now ready to use! You can use it as an ingredient, an elixir, or as a topping on your favorite yogurt, salad, or baked good. Use as your desire commands.

Personalizing Your Oxymels

As you experiment with creating oxymels, you may want to adjust the ratio of honey and vinegar to your personal taste and the herbs according to their efficacy. Other herbs you may wish to experiment with are horehound, rosemary, or sage. If you are new to herbalism, stick with tonic herbs, as these are very safe. Use your grimoire to record your process so that when you discover and create the perfect recipe, you will be able to re-create it.

PART II

100 MAGICKAL HERBS

This part includes thorough information about one hundred of the most-often-used herbs in witchcraft and magick. You'll find yourself turning to these herbs again and again to help you connect with the earth; heal and balance your body, mind, and spirit; and offer blessings and gratitude. Locate important information quickly and easily with this alphabetized list of herbs, which includes their common name, scientific name, history, characteristics, and magickal properties.

Allspice

(Pimenta dioica)

History
Christopher Columbus is dubiously credited
with "discovering" allspice in Jamaica, which
most likely means that he discovered indigenous
people using it first. Its documented use dates
back to the late 1400s. It is native to the Carib-
bean islands, Mexico, and other parts of Central
America.

Characteristics
Allspice is sometimes called pimento because it resembles pepper-
corn. Its aroma and flavor bear a strong resemblance to nutmeg, cinnamon, clove, and ginger; hence the name allspice. Allspice grows on
small evergreen trees, and its seeds are spread mainly by birds. The
dried berries are used as a culinary ingredient, as a perfume, and even
as a natural pesticide.

Magickal Properties
Allspice is an herb of increase and is often used to attract money and
wealth. The berries can be used as an herbal talisman on their own or
as part of a charm. In your spellwork, use allspice along with whatever it is you want to increase.

Aloe Vera

(Aloe vera)

History
Native to Africa, the physical healing powers of
aloe vera are well documented. Legend states
that Alexander the Great arranged treatment
for his legion of soldiers with aloe vera when they were injured.
The Egyptian queen Cleopatra is reported to have used aloe vera as
part of her beauty routine. Aloe vera was indeed a sacred plant to the
ancient Egyptians, as is evidenced by the inclusion of aloe vera in the

paintings that adorned the walls of the temples, conferring religious symbolism to this succulent plant.

Characteristics

The aloe vera plant has green or green and white variegated leaves with small spines on the outer edges. The most common parts used are the leaves and the gel contained within them. Aloe vera gel is often used to treat burns and other skin irritations but is also found in cosmetic products such as shampoo and toothpaste. Aloe vera is also an edible plant with sap that is known to soothe upset stomachs.

Magickal Properties

The Latin *vera* is the feminine form of "true," making the spiny leaves of the aloe vera plant useful in spells designed to halt gossip. Because of its soothing nature, aloe can also be used in healing spells.

Angelica

(Angelica archangelica)

History

Native to Europe, angelica has been cultivated since ancient times for its roots, leaves, and seeds. Its recorded use dates back to the tenth century when it was used as an aromatic, a medicinal, and an edible.

Characteristics

Angelica is an aromatic relative of parsley, with dark green serrated leaves and flowers that grow in spherical clusters from a single long stem. Angelica is also related to the carrot— their similarities can be seen in angelica's root structure, which can grow up to 10 feet deep. It is a carminative herb, a diuretic, and an expectorant. The roots and leaves of the angelica plant are used in tinctures; however, the fresh root has toxic qualities and must be thoroughly dried before decocting. The essential oil made from angelica has been used as a topical treatment for inflammation of the joints. The leaves are sometimes used as a topical as well as a tea. Angelica is very powerful and should be avoided by expectant mothers and children.

Magickal Properties

The pagan associations of angelica have to do with the rites of spring. So strong were the magickal implications of angelica (such as its ability to protect against evil), that, like many of the pagan sabbats, angelica was adopted by Christians as a holy herb. Referred to as "the Root of the Holy Ghost" according to Opal Streisand in her book *Sacred Herbs*, angelica was believed to bloom on the feast day of the archangel Michael and to ward against evil and, ironically, witchcraft. Angelica was also believed to cure the plague, according to a monk who was given this information by an angel.

Arnica

(Arnica fulgens)

History

Discovered by Europeans during the late 1500s, arnica was also used by Native Americans, but it is not known when arnica became known in indigenous American culture. The entire plant was used, right down to the roots. Later, the use of arnica was refined so that just the flowers were used as a tincture or topical. They grow in meadows and are native to the mountain regions of America and Europe.

Characteristics

Arnica is a perennial member of the Asteraceae family. Its bright orange-yellow flowers resemble that of a daisy. Arnica is widely known for its healing properties. Used as a topical, it has a beneficial effect on bruises, aches, and sprains.

Magickal Properties

Arnica represents strength due to its association with mountainous regions. It can be used to invoke the power of the oreades, the mountain nymphs of ancient Greece. Arnica can be used as an altar offering to invoke vitality or carried in a sachet for inner strength.

Barberry or Common Barberry

(Mahonia aquifolium or Berberis vulgaris)

History
Barberry was used by Native Americans, primarily as an appetite stimulant. This was noted by early European colonists, who had used barberry as a bitter tonic to treat digestive problems.

Characteristics
Barberry is sometimes referred to as Oregon grape. Barberry is a lush evergreen shrub with dark bluish-black berries. Varieties grow 2–4 feet high. The bark of the roots and stems is used.

Magickal Properties
Barberry's magickal associations are clearing, cleansing, and letting go. Barberry berries can also be used in banishing spells. The roots of common barberry can be used in spells to increase psychic vision.

Basil

(Ocimum basilicum)

History
Basil has been enjoyed for four to five thousand years. In ancient Greece, it was referred to as a "royal herb," most likely because the etymology is connected to *basileus*, which is the Greek word for "king." It is also associated with divinity in Hinduism, where it is revered. In the Greek Orthodox religion, basil is used as a purifying herb in the preparation of holy water. In Europe, it is also a sacred offering to the dead. Bundles of basil are sometimes placed in the hands of the deceased in order to assure them of a safe passage to the spirit realm.

Characteristics

Part of the mint family, basil is highly aromatic and is used as an ornamental herb as well as a popular culinary herb. It is a perennial low-growing herb with light green glossy leaves and white flowers. Basil enjoys warm, dry conditions.

Magickal Properties

Basil is a symbol of love and happiness. It cultivates strength and has protective properties as well. It is often used in spells for money, love, and luck as well as for predicting the state of romantic relationships or marriages. Author Scott Cunningham tells of a predictive spell where two basil leaves are placed on a hot coal and the reaction of the leaves symbolizes the health of the relationship. Leaves that turn to ash indicate a successful partnership, while leaves that hiss indicate marital strife.

Bayberry
(Myrica pensylvanica)

History

Infusion of bayberry root bark was used in folk medicine as a healing tonic. Also used as a poultice, bayberry was used as a treatment for ulcers and stomach ailments, even though it is an emetic. Bayberry contains tannin and is not recommended for consumption today.

Characteristics

Bayberry is a large evergreen shrub. Also known as southern bayberry, varieties of this plant are closely related to the wax myrtle. Bayberry berries are bluish-white in appearance.

Magickal Properties

Bayberry is a Yuletide herb used in candle magick. Bayberry candles are lit during the winter solstice to herald the return of the light. Bayberry berries produce a waxy substance with a pleasant aroma.

Belladonna
(Atropa bella-donna)

History

Historically, belladonna has been associated
with witches, as it was an ingredient listed
in a medieval "flying ointment." It has also
been used for military purposes, both as a poisoning agent as well as
an antidote. The poisonous juice of *Atropa bella-donna* was used by the
Scottish army to intoxicate and incapacitate the Norwegian troops of
King Svein Knutsson, who attempted to take Scotland from Duncan
the First. *Atropa bella-donna* was also strategically used in World War
II by the Allied forces. Atropine, an alkaloid derived from belladonna,
was the only known antidote to the nerve gas used by Germany. Belladonna is a dangerous herb. Sacred to the Fates, belladonna is associated with Atropos, the Fate who cuts the thread of life. Belladonna
was also believed to take the form of a woman who was beautiful but
dangerous to meet.

Characteristics

Belladonna is a poisonous plant with a rigid stalk that grows into
branches. A perennial plant, belladonna can grow up to 3 feet tall. Its
flowers are shaped like bells and have a purplish-brown color. The berries are black, about the size of cherries, with lots of seeds and juice as
dark as ink. Belladonna can grow in partial shade in chalky soil.

Magickal Properties

Belladonna is used magickally for seduction and the amplification of
visions. A potently poisonous herb, it should not be ingested. Berries can be included in a scrying charm by folding the dried berry
within a sigil and placing the charm on the scrying mirror to charge
it with the intention on the sigil for what you wish to see. Because of
belladonna's association with attraction, it is tempting to use in love
magick; however, remember that the flowers of belladonna are solitary and its power is in the temporary illusion of beauty. Seduction
and love are not the same thing.

Bergamot

(Monarda didyma)

History

Bergamot is cultivated across the United States, Central America, Europe, and Asia. Before it was spread to the world by the colonial invaders of the indigenous people's land, it was referred to as Oswego tea. Attractive to bees and possessing a citrus-like, minty taste, the flowers and leaves of bergamot have been used as a remedy and a tea before and throughout colonization of the native land presently known as the United States. Bergamot is also known as beebalm, scarlet beebalm, and crimson bee balm.

Characteristics

Grown throughout North America, bergamot is often planted with the goal of attracting bees and butterflies, which are drawn to its citrus scent. Its long, hollow, pipe-shaped flowers are attractive to hummingbirds. It is widely used as a flavoring and in teas.

Magickal Properties

Bergamot is used for prosperity spells and binding spells, as well as for protection and invoking luck. Because it is associated with the planet Venus, bergamot is also used in love magick.

Betony

(Stachys officinalis)

History

Appearing in Italian and Spanish folklore, betony was a widely used remedy believed to be effective for almost everything. Ancient Romans believed that betony could cure no less than forty-seven distinct diseases.

Characteristics

Native to Europe and cultivated extensively in herb gardens, betony is a perennial plant with pink or purple flowers. Growing up to 3 feet, betony has spiky stems and hairy leaves that grow in a rosette pattern.

In the wild, betony grows in meadows enjoying full sun. The entire aerial portion of the plant is used for its astringent effects.

Magickal Properties

Used since the Middle Ages in magick, betony was believed to give protection against evil spirits. Sprigs of betony left on the windowsills or hung in doorways cast a protective charm over the inhabitants and contents of a home.

Black Cohosh

(Cimicifuga racemosa)

History

Native Americans introduced the use of black cohosh for the treatment of sprains, fevers, and coughs or pneumonia. European colonists used the herb as a remedy for irregular menstrual cycles. Black cohosh was also used as an insect repellant.

Characteristics

Black cohosh is easy to cultivate and fares well in sunny gardens. Black cohosh also does well in shade, as it is often found growing wild in woodlands. Though it has beautiful flowers, they have a very unappealing odor. The decocted root is used as a remedy to stimulate menstruation. Other names for black cohosh are bugbane, bugwort, rattleweed, and black snakeroot.

Magickal Properties

Black cohosh is used for banishing spells. To rid yourself or your surroundings of unwanted energy, add drops of black cohosh tincture to a spray bottle with equal parts distilled water and witch hazel and use the mixture to clear a space or even to purge energy from items. Add three drops of an essential oil such as sage to amplify the spell.

Bloodroot
(Sanguinaria canadensis)

History
Bloodroot is native to the eastern United States. The Algonquin Ojibwe tribe was said to have used the bloodroot rhizome (root) as a remedy for coughs. Bloodroot was also used as a dye.

Characteristics
Bloodroot's name is a reference to the reddish-orange color of its root, and it can be cultivated in gardens by dividing the root stems, which is easier than propagating this herb from seed. Bloodroot prefers to grow in sheltered, mossy areas. Its beautiful white flowers are ephemeral, lasting only a few days. The seed dispersal of bloodroot is dependent on ants.

Magickal Properties
Bloodroot is used in relationship spells. It can strengthen an existing bond or be used to inject an element of change into an existing relationship.

Blue Cohosh
(Caulophyllum thalictroides)

History
Blue cohosh has been used by Native Americans for hundreds of years to stimulate menstrual flow and even labor. It is one of the oldest-known indigenous medicinal remedies. It was introduced into Western medicine through a book by Peter Smith in 1813. Because of Smith's publication, the western settlers of the United States of non-native origin were able to apply the remedies used by the original inhabitants.

Characteristics

Blue cohosh is a perennial herb that grows around 1–3 feet tall. Its flowers are yellowish light green. The plant changes color as it matures. It starts out as purple, then blooms into yellowish green. As it matures, its colors change once again to an unusual bluish-green. Its berries are dark blue.

Magickal Properties

Blue cohosh is used for endings. If you want the strength to end a relationship and need to craft a breakup charm, crush the fruit of blue cohosh with barberry to strengthen your resolve.

Boneset

(Eupatorium perfoliatum)

History

The use of boneset dates back to the time of Mithridates Eupator, an ancient king of Pontus (near present-day Turkey), who is credited with using the boneset herb as a medicinal. Boneset is known to induce perspiration to relieve fever and even nausea and to purge toxins. It held official drug status until 1950, although it was rarely prescribed by allopathic practitioners.

Characteristics

Part of the daisy family, boneset is a perennial herb known for its hardiness. Boneset grows to around 5 feet and has a hairy stem that culminates with white tube-shaped florets. Historically, it was used to treat fevers, not broken bones, as its name would suggest.

Magickal Properties

Boneset is an emetic herb and can be magickally used in spells that mark an ending, letting go, parting of the ways, or the dissolution of a partnership.

Borage

(Borago officinalis)

History
Although borage is native to Syria, it was the Romans who introduced it to the rest of the countries along the Mediterranean Sea. In the first century C.E., borage is mentioned by both Pliny the Elder and Dioscorides as a source of courage and happiness.

Characteristics
The flowers, leaves, and seeds of the borage plant are used in tea, oils, infusions, compresses, and poultices. Borage grows to a height of around 2 feet, has a salty taste, and is thought to resemble cucumbers in its flavor.

Magickal Properties
The pentacle motif of borage has earned it the nickname "star flower." Borage is considered to be an uplifting herb, and its magickal applications include mood elevation and the cultivation of courage. Borage can be used to amplify your personal energy when strength and bravery are required. The gifts of borage are happiness and strength.

Broom

(Cytisus scoparius)

History
Broom was a popular garden plant from the mid-1800s through the twentieth century. Introduced on the East Coast, it later spread across the United States. Historically, broom was used to flavor beer and to tan leather. In the mid-twentieth century, broom gained a reputation for being an intoxicant when smoked, but this practice is not recommended now.

The Modern Witchcraft Guide to Magickal Herbs

Characteristics

Broom is a shrub with large, bright yellow flowers, and it grows along the Atlantic Coast as well as the Pacific Northwest. It flourishes in the full sunlight and can tolerate a variety of soil conditions. It is both an ornamental and an invasive plant. It is very resilient, with seeds that can remain viable for many years.

Magickal Properties

Also known as broom tops and Scotch broom, this herb was embraced by the counterculture as a conduit to euphoria and psychic awareness. Broom can be used magickally in the seeing of auras as well as chakra alignment, as it has associations with enhancing the perception of color. Branches can be gathered and bundled together and burned as incense. The flowering tops can be infused in water and used for anointing or as an asperge.

Burdock
(Arctium lappa)

History

Grown intentionally for its edible roots in Asia, burdock is considered a weed elsewhere. Its Latin binomial is derived from the Greek word for "bear" and the Celtic word *llap*, which means "to seize," which no doubt refers to its problematic seeds (see Characteristics).

Characteristics

A large, biennial herb, burdock is nutritive and versatile, with almost all of its parts cited for uses in folk medicine to strengthen the immune system. The roots, seeds, leaves, and flower stems are rich in vitamins and minerals. Burdock is characterized by its seed pods, which are notorious for getting caught on just about everything and are difficult and painful to remove—in fact, they are the inspiration for Velcro. Burdock is a biennial plant with a two-year life cycle.

Magickal Properties

Burdock has many folk names, including cockle bur, beggar's buttons, and clotbur. Wandering into a burdock patch is considered bad luck because of the seed pods. It is used ritually for purification and as an amplifier, lending power to spells invoking transformation. Burdock can also be used in binding spells, such as to hinder an undesirable outcome. Burdock root can also be threaded with string and worn as a charm.

Butcher's-Broom

(Ruscus aculeatus)

History

Butcher's-broom was referenced by Dioscorides in the first century as a laxative, while Culpeper suggested it be used for the healing of broken bones.

Characteristics

Also known as knee holly or box holly, butcher's-broom is a diminutive evergreen shrub. It is native to the Mediterranean region but grows throughout the Pacific Northwest and is recognized by its yellow flowers and red berries. Butcher's-broom has tough stems that allow it to live up to its name.

Magickal Properties

Use butcher's-broom in clearing rituals. Whether you are reclaiming sacred space or need to fortify personal boundaries, making an herbal charm with butcher's-broom will amplify your quest for clarity.

Calamus

(Acorus calamus)

History

Also known as sweet flag, calamus has been used as a remedy for fevers and as a culinary herb dating back to biblical times. Today, however, it's no longer used for those purposes.

The Modern Witchcraft Guide to Magickal Herbs

Characteristics

Calamus is a perennial herb that prefers wetland environments. Growing near ponds, lakes, swamps, and streams throughout the mid-latitude continents, calamus flowers resemble those of the iris.

Magickal Properties

Calamus is used for uncrossing spells. It can also be used for divination in scrying. Sprinkle a little of the dried herb on your altar and set your scrying tool (mirror or crystal) on top of it if you want to reveal things as they are and not as they seem.

Calendula

(Calendula officinalis)

History

Calendula is cited in both the Ayurvedic tradition as well as in traditional Chinese medicine. In medieval times, calendula was regarded as a magickal herb as well as a medicinal and culinary. Used ritually in the classical Greco-Roman world, calendula is seen in the garlands that adorn deities of the Hindu faith as well as in offerings to ancestors on the Day of the Dead in Central America. For the Romans, calendula was a symbol of joy.

Characteristics

The bright yellow flowers of the calendula plant have been used to produce dye, to flavor food, and even to impart an attractive yellow hue to cheese. Calendula is native to southern Europe and takes its name from "calends," also known as the first of the month in the ancient Roman calendar. The blossoms of *Calendula officinalis* open in the morning and follow the sun, closing in the late afternoon.

Magickal Properties

Calendula is among the most spiritually significant herbs. Garlands of calendula are used as a protective charm. The blossoms are used for protections against nightmares.

Capsicum

(Capsicum annuum)

History
Capsicum, also known as cayenne pepper or chili pepper, has been widely cultivated for centuries for seasoning and also as a vermifuge (a way to kill parasites).

Characteristics
Proliferate cultivation has yielded many different varieties and potencies of capsicum. Size, shape, and pungency are dependent on the specific type of variety. Colors range from green to yellow, orange, and red. The fruit can grow from 1 to 6 inches in length.

Magickal Properties
Capsicum can be used magickally in a variety of spells from silencing a witness in court to serious protection magick. Used as a banishing agent in root work, capsicum has also been implicated in Central American maleficio magick due to its potential for harm.

Catnip

(Nepeta cataria)

History
Cats have long held an affinity for this herb, but it has also been used historically as a medicine, as it is a carminative herb to relieve gas. Its use has been attributed to ancient Romans, Native Americans, and European colonists.

Characteristics
The flowering tops of this common perennial herb induce playfulness in cats. Catnip grows in proliferation along the edges of paths and roads. It is pleasant-tasting and is also used as a sleep aid. Originating in Europe, Asia, and Africa, catnip is now grown throughout the world.

Magickal Properties

Catnip is used to invoke predictive dreams. Ancient Egyptians made offerings of catnip to Bast, a goddess who took on a feline form. Catnip is also used in magick as an aid to overcoming ordeals. When faced with a particularly difficult challenge, drinking an infusion of catnip or wearing a sprig either fresh or dried in a charm will make obstacles easier to overcome.

Chamomile

(Chamaemelum nobile)

History

A traditional medicinal, chamomile originates from western Europe, India, and Asia. Its earliest recorded use was as a treatment for fevers by the Egyptians. Also known as English or Roman chamomile, it is so widely used throughout Europe that it is considered a cure-all. Chamomile was revered by the ancient Egyptians and was frequently used in offerings to the gods.

Characteristics

Chamomile is a low-growing perennial that reaches no more than 10 inches in height. Known for its calming effect, chamomile is also a bitter herb that can aid in the digestion of fats and thereby soothe the stomach. Chamomile has many varieties, including German, Hungarian, Roman, and English.

Magickal Properties

The garden variety of chamomile is believed to be a healing presence to other plants, earning chamomile the nickname of the "plant's physician." It is also used in luck and money-drawing spells.

Chickweed

(Stellaria media)

History
Described in the past as a useful demulcent (something that reduces inflammation near a mucous membrane) and diuretic, chickweed is mostly considered a weed. It does have nutritional value, so it is used as feed for chickens and other birds.

Characteristics
Chickweed is a low-growing perennial edible plant with small, white star-shaped flowers. The leaves and stems are used in salad and cooked greens. It grows in large mats with several plants emanating from the underground taproots. Chickweed is a harbinger of the spring planting season.

Magickal Properties
Chickweed is used in healing spells; its white flowers represent purity and clarity. Because it is edible, consuming the leaves allows you to take the associated energy internally and thereby invoke transformation. Chickweed can also be used in protection spells and as a ward to keep away unwanted energies.

Chicory

(Cichorium intybus)

History
Native to Europe, chicory is widely associated with New Orleans, a city steeped in witchcraft. It is valued in folk medicine and has been used historically as a poultice for inflammations, as well as a culinary green.

Characteristics
Also known as succory, chicory is a perennial member of the daisy family. It grows to around 3 feet in height. Its roasted root is fre-

quently used as an additive to coffee, while its leaves are used in salads and cooked greens. Its attractive blue flowers can be spotted growing wild across North America.

Magickal Properties
Chicory is used in love magick. If you find yourself becoming too involved or overly preoccupied with a love interest, carrying chicory can help bring you back to center.

Chrysanthemum
(Chrysanthemum morifolium)

History
Cultivated in China, there are references to chrysanthemums dating back to the fifteenth century B.C.E., according to the National Chrysanthemum Society. Its roots, leaves, and flowers were used both medicinally and in culinary ways: Roots were indicated as treatment for headaches, while infusions of the leaves and flowers made a refreshing and celebratory drink. The chrysanthemum is considered one of the four noble plants in Chinese literature, alongside bamboo, plum blossom, and orchid. Chrysanthemum is also called *Dios ophyra*, meaning "God's eyebrow." In Italy, chrysanthemum is associated with the dead due to its ability to bloom in low-light conditions and because it blooms in autumn, which is the season of Samhain.

Characteristics
Chrysanthemum is believed to increase circulation. Infusion of chrysanthemum has been used to address ailments such as cold and flu symptoms, as it reduces fever and chills. It is also used to treat headaches and dizziness.

Magickal Properties
Chrysanthemum symbolizes optimism, happiness, and joy. Dew collected from the petals promotes longevity.

Coltsfoot

(Tussilago farfara)

History

Folk traditions have cited coltsfoot as a demulcent, or a soothing agent; however, recent studies have discouraged its use. Coltsfoot was historically used to treat coughs before it was discovered to be unsafe for medical purposes.

Characteristics

Coltsfoot is a perennial herb that grows low to the ground. Its texture can be described as woolly. Coltsfoot blooms in the spring, sending up a stem that culminates in a single yellow blossom. Native to Europe, coltsfoot prefers places that are sandy and moist. It grows throughout southern Canada, as well as the northeast and north-central United States.

Magickal Properties

The magickal use of coltsfoot is derived from its hoof-shaped leaves. A charm of dried coltsfoot leaves can be used to hasten the arrival of a message or as an offering to Rhiannon, the Welsh goddess of the moon. Often depicted with or as a horse, Rhiannon is also associated with the faerie folk as well as with prophetic dreams.

Comfrey

(Symphytum officinale)

History

Although it grows throughout North America, comfrey is native to Asia and Europe. Primarily used for its leaves and roots, comfrey is associated with numerous healing properties including broken bones, gums, and teeth, as well as boosting the immune system. It is used as a topical and has been called "bruisewort" due to its efficacy in contributing to the healing of minor surface injuries. One of its common names was "knitbone" because it was used as a poultice and applied topically to reduce the swelling around broken bones.

Characteristics

Attracted to water, comfrey can be found growing wild near rivers and ponds. It can reach 6 feet in height and is characterized by its hairy stalk and purplish-pink flowers. Its leaves are dark green with deep veins. Comfrey has an air of controversy surrounding it due to medical studies that attributed liver damage in lab rats to the vast amounts of comfrey they were fed. Comfrey is not ingested, but is widely used in topicals for the skin to treat inflammations and also as an astringent and an analgesic.

Magickal Properties

Magickal associations of comfrey include protection, setting boundaries, and associations with time. Ruled by Saturn, comfrey is associated with slow growth. Use comfrey in spells when your intention is set on manifesting long-term goals.

Coriander

(Coriandrum sativum)

History

Native to the Mediterranean region, coriander seeds have been discovered in ancient ruins. Used for millennia, coriander is documented all the way back to 5000 B.C.E. Its feathery leaves resemble parsley, and its potent aroma and flavor have made it somewhat of a polarizing herb.

Characteristics

The leaves and seeds of coriander have been used as a remedy for colic. Coriander seeds are also used to treat nausea, diarrhea, and flatulence. Its growth cycle runs from March to September, with the best time for harvesting leaves occurring in late spring to autumn. It is an annual herb, and the entire plant is edible.

Magickal Properties

Coriander is so esteemed in Chinese medicine that it has even been associated with immortality—that is why coriander seeds can be used as offerings to the dead on Samhain. They are also included in love charms to attract a love interest, boost fertility, and protect fidelity. Seeds can be sewn into a red pouch and carried in a pocket or worn on the body.

Cranberry

(Vaccinium macrocarpon)

History

In the early twentieth century, scientists made
an association between the consumption of cran-
berry and a reduction in urinary tract infections in women. While
initially believed to be attributed to cranberry's acidic effects, it was
later proven to be a combination of several compounds in cranberry
that achieved this outcome.

Characteristics

Cultivated extensively, cranberry favors the bogs of the northeast-
ern United States. It is produced commercially in Massachusetts and
Washington in both natural and human-made bogs. Cranberry has
ellipse-shaped evergreen leaves with a waxy appearance. The distinct
dark pink flowers are followed by the dark red berries, which measure
around ½ inch in diameter.

Magickal Properties

Cranberries ripen in late fall, aligning them with the waning year and
the energies of the crone goddess. Use dried cranberries in a charm
to honor the wisdom of the elders or as an offering to the ancestors.

Damiana

(Turnera diffusa)

History

Damiana was introduced to America as
an aphrodisiac in 1874. Touted as a pelvic
toner, virility amplifier, and fertility aid
by an American pharmacist, damiana's reputation as an herb of sexual
enhancement persisted well past the point when its chemical properties were discovered to have no impact on sexual function. It does
contain complex volatile oils, which account for its taste and aroma,
both of which are associated with sensuality.

Characteristics

Native to Mexico, damiana is a leafy shrub. The leaves have been used in tinctures and combined with other ingredients in tonic preparations and also used in infusions.

Magickal Properties

Still used in love magick, damiana leaves are included in charms designed to summon the object of affection and as a magickal restorative to existing relationships in need of rejuvenation.

Dandelion

(Taraxacum officinale)

History

Named for the appearance of its leaves, which are said to resemble the "tooth of the lion," the use of dandelion has been extant since the days of ancient Rome. It is believed that European settlers intentionally brought dandelions to North America primarily as a source of medicine. Dandelion is associated with Belenos, the Celtic sun god, most likely due to its bright yellow flowers, whose thin and narrow petals are reminiscent of the rays of the sun.

Characteristics

Dandelion is a perennial plant that enjoys moisture and full sun. It is used in wine, medicine, and food. Dandelion has a 10- to 15-inch taproot, which facilitates its propagation. A dandelion can regenerate even if it retains only a small portion of its taproot. It is easily identified by its feathery clocks, those unmistakable white puffballs that distribute its seeds on the wind. Its long, green serrated leaves range from 3 to 12 inches in length, radiating from a center point in a rosette shape. It grows well in all northern temperate zones.

Magickal Properties

A dream of a dandelion is a harbinger of difficult times ahead, according to druidic lore. These changes and challenges, however, can eventually have positive effects. When the dandelion blossom is in its post-flowering state, the clocks can be used for the divination of love.

Devil's Claw

(Harpagophytum procumbens)

History

Devil's claw was used in Africa as an aid to women in childbirth. It is also cited as an herb that can terminate a pregnancy, but this claim has not been scientifically verified. In native African folk medicine, devil's claw was described as a wonder drug for myriad health ailments as well as change-of-life issues, such as menopause. It is still used widely throughout Europe as a digestive aid and an appetite stimulant.

Characteristics

Also referred to as "wood spider" and "grapple plant," devil's claw is named for the unusual appearance of its fruit, which is covered with what appears to be tiny hooks. Native to South Africa, the use of devil's claw has been cited in a wide variety of remedies for everything from arthritis and other inflammations to allergies and diseases of filter organs such as the liver and kidneys.

Magickal Properties

Devil's claw can be used magickally to attract or repel, depending on the intention of the practitioner. As a summoning charm, devil's claw can amplify that which you seek to call to yourself or to increase desire.

Echinacea

(Echinacea angustifolia, pallida, and purpurea)

History

Native Americans have purportedly used echinacea as a cure for a variety of ailments for over four hundred years. It has been associated with indigenous American tribes including the Cheyenne, Choctaw, Comanche, and Dakota Sioux.

Characteristics

Echinacea is a perennial plant that grows 2–4 feet tall. It is recognizable by its bright purple cone flowers. It is tolerant of droughts and is used as an immune booster as well as a treatment for cold and flu symptoms. Echinacea has been widely scrutinized for its efficacy, particularly for its anti-inflammatory and antibacterial characteristics. Echinacea is also attractive to bees, butterflies, and birds.

Magickal Properties

Seeds of the echinacea plant are used in spells for abundance as well as fertility. It is also used as an amplifier and an opener of psychic doors to perception.

Elder

(Sambucus nigra)

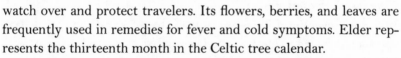

History

Originating from northwestern Europe, the elder tree is held sacred by numerous cultures. Elder trees were also believed to watch over and protect travelers. Its flowers, berries, and leaves are frequently used in remedies for fever and cold symptoms. Elder represents the thirteenth month in the Celtic tree calendar.

Characteristics

The elder tree produces clusters of dark bluish-black berries that are used for fever reduction, respiratory health, the treatment of diarrhea, and inflammation of the joints.

Magickal Properties

Elder is used as both a blessing and a ward. Hung over a doorway in bundles, it promotes prosperity for those dwelling within the house and staves off bad fortune so that it does not cross the threshold. The elder also represents the crone aspect of the triple goddess. Because of its association with the crone, elder represents the veil between the earthly people and their relations and ancestors in the spiritual realm.

Evening Primrose

(Oenothera biennis)

History

Used by early European settlers as well as Native Americans, evening primrose was introduced to what is now the United States in the early seventeenth century. It was used to treat coughs, bruises, and digestive ailments. It is believed to have been brought to the Americas on the ballasts of ships, to which its seeds adhered.

Characteristics

Evening primrose is considered a weed in North America. It is a biennial herb noted for its prolific seed production. Native Americans would use the whole plant as a remedy for coughs and also as a topical for treating minor injuries such as bruises. The oil from the seeds contains chemicals that are medically recognized in the treatment of premenstrual syndrome as well as promoting breast health.

Magickal Properties

In magick, evening primrose is used for manifesting abundance. It is considered sacred to hunters and is used to draw your desires into being. The crepe-y yellow flowers have a touch of iridescence to them, giving the blossoms a mystical and lunar energy.

Eyebright

(Euphrasia officinalis)

History

During the Renaissance, eyebright was often combined with tobacco and smoked as an expectorant. It was also popular when made into an elixir such as ale, as well as a topical. Juice from eyebright was used to heal eye afflictions.

Characteristics

The leaves, flowers, and stems of eyebright are used to address colds and other minor health afflictions. Eyebright is used in infusions, compresses, tinctures, and capsules to soothe ailments such as symptoms of allergies or as a remedy for common cold indicators. Eyebright is a small annual plant with white or purplish flowers that feature yellow spots and stripes.

Magickal Properties

Eyebright brings with it radiant goddess energy. Named for Euphrosyne, one of the three Graces or Charities of Greek mythology, eyebright is said to bring joy. Eyebright has angelic associations, as John Milton wrote in *Paradise Lost* that the archangel Michael used eyebright to cure an eye affliction that troubled Adam after he ate the false fruit.

Fennel

(Foeniculum vulgare)

History

Used in ancient Rome as a remedy, Pliny the Elder attributed no less than twenty-two benefits to fennel. His observations even included that fennel was consumed by snakes when they were undergoing molting. Pliny also believed that it sharpened their eyesight.

Characteristics

Fennel is used for its roots, seeds, and leaves. It is a culinary herb, and the shoots and bulbs are edible. It is also used as a purgative. Fennel is a tall perennial herb, growing up to 5 feet, with feathery leaves that resemble fine thread. The fruit of the fennel herb is quite small and is often referred to as seeds.

Magickal Properties

Fennel is a protective herb. Bundles of fennel hung over a doorway were used in medieval times as a ward against evil. In modern witchcraft, it is used to ward off unwanted interference, such as nosy neighbors. When eaten, fennel seeds sweeten the breath and as such promote kindness and friendship.

Fenugreek

(Trigonella foenum-graecum)

History
Lydia Pinkham included fenugreek in
her famed Vegetable Compound, which
was a popular women's tonic in the
1800s. It was rumored to promote fertility as well as address a host
of women's issues from menstruation to menopause.

Characteristics
This small European herb is sometimes referred to as Greek hayseed.
The seeds are used externally in poultices and ointments. Fenugreek
has a taste likened to maple syrup. Its flavor is pleasant and its effects
are soothing.

Magickal Properties
Fenugreek is used in spells of abundance and protections. When the
seeds are scattered, they are considered a blessing upon the dwelling
that stands upon the land. Fenugreek infusions have also been used
in apotropaic magick ("apotropaic," meaning "able to ward off evil");
that's why washing with fenugreek infusion will dispel bad luck.

Feverfew

(Tanacetum parthenium)

History
Feverfew has been in use since the time of Dioscorides in the first century c.e. It has been used
to treat fevers, headaches, stomachaches, and
irregular menstrual cycles. In the 1970s, feverfew was used as an alternative therapy for people
suffering from migraines.

Characteristics
Feverfew is a perennial herb with a strong aroma. Fresh leaves, dried
leaves, and powdered leaves have all been shown to reduce the fre-
quency of severe headaches.

Magickal Properties

Feverfew is used as a purifying herb and also as a countercharm. It can be used to consecrate magickal tools and to break binding spells.

Garlic

(Allium sativum)

History

Garlic has been used as a remedy and as a culinary herb since the dawn of history. The bulbs as well as the stems and leaves, known as scapes, have been cited in over 125 different treatments.

Characteristics

Part of the lily family, the bulbs of the garlic plant have been used as a remedy for a variety of ailments ranging from blood pressure issues to stomach ailments. When the bulbs are consumed fresh or freeze-dried in enteric-coated capsules, the most effective health benefits are gained.

Magickal Properties

A powerful apotropaic herb, garlic has been used as a ward against vampires, demons, and black magick. It is also used as an aphrodisiac. Garlic can repel or attract depending on the intent and will of the practitioner.

Gentian

(Gentiana lutea)

History

Gentian root has been used for over two thousand years and is mentioned by Pliny the Elder in *Naturalis Historia*. It is believed to have been named after an ancient king of Illyria, Gentius, who ruled from 181 B.C.E. until 168 B.C.E., when he was defeated by the Romans. Gentius purportedly discovered the medicinal uses of *Gentiana lutea*.

Characteristics

Gentian is a tall, flowering herb with a sturdy stem and clusters of bright orange and yellow flowers. Native to central and southern Europe, gentian grows in the alpine and subalpine meadows. It is the main ingredient in Angostura bitters. The root of the plant is used. It takes several years for the gentian root to mature.

Magickal Properties

Gentian root is used in love magick. Chips of the dried root can be added to an incense blend and burned to attract love, or it can be carried in a sachet or pouch.

Ginger

(Zingiber officinale)

History

Ginger has been used for more than 2,500 years. Its consumption began in China, and it is now valued throughout the world for its flavor. Ginger is a key part of Chinese medicine in that it is an effective digestive aid and also soothes the stomach, easing ailments such as nausea.

Characteristics

The rhizome, or underground stem, is the part of the plant that is typically used. Ginger is commonly referred to as Jamaica ginger, African ginger, or Cochin ginger, depending on its origin. It is a pungent herb and has been studied extensively. It has been shown to reduce the symptoms of motion sickness.

Magickal Properties

Root of ginger hung in a doorway is a magickal ward used to protect women in childbirth. Ginger root buried near an entryway protects the home. Wine steeped in ginger has been used as a love potion. Ginger is also associated with longevity and immortality.

Ginkgo

(Ginkgo biloba)

History

Ginkgo is one of the oldest living trees in the world today, having survived since the Paleolithic era. Ginkgo trees can purportedly live for thousands of years, with some trees believed to be 2,500 years old. Ginkgo is important in traditional Chinese medicine and is often cited for its beneficial effects on memory as well as sexual function.

Characteristics

Ginkgo trees are remarkably hardy and can tolerate cold climates and even the stress of cities. Ginkgo can thrive in urban environments. It is also called the "maidenhair tree" in England because its leaves are similar in appearance to the maidenhair fern, which is native to western Europe. It is distinguished by its fan-shaped, notched leaves. The nut of the ginkgo tree is used to increase virility and also as a treatment for asthma.

Magickal Properties

Ginkgo is used in sex magick and also as a spell amplifier. It is symbolic of the wisdom of the ages due to its longevity.

Goldenseal

(Hydrastis canadensis)

History

Goldenseal was used by Native Americans as a dye as well as for its medicinal properties. In the 1800s, European colonists adopted its use as an eyewash and a tonic, contributing to goldenseal's popularity. In folk medicine, goldenseal has been recommended for healing the mouth and lips.

Characteristics

Goldenseal is difficult to cultivate. Each seedling takes two to four years to develop a mature root. It takes five years before goldenseal can be harvested. A perennial plant, goldenseal prefers moist, wooded areas. Overharvesting has led goldenseal to become very rare. It is considered endangered in six US states.

Magickal Properties

Magickal applications include enhanced communication and healing from disagreements. Goldenseal can be used in spells to repair the damage done by harsh words or gossip.

Hawthorn

(Crataegus laevigata)

History

The hawthorn is regarded as a magickal tree throughout western Europe. It is associated with the heart, love, and lust. Its flowers are believed to have an aphrodisiac aroma. The flowers, leaves, and berries were used as a tonic benefiting circulation and regulating blood pressure, making hawthorn's association with the heart medicinal and magickal.

Characteristics

The hawthorn is a small- to medium-sized tree with thorny branches. It can reach upward of 30 feet in height. Hawthorn is characterized by its thorns, which are about an inch long. The hawthorn flowers in May, making it a harbinger of Beltane. After the spring, flowers give rise to fruit. The hawthorn is identified by its bright red berries, which last until winter.

Magickal Properties

Hawthorn is considered a magickal tree. When it grows alongside oak and ash, this place is believed to be sacred to faeries. Hawthorn played an integral part in the rites of Beltane and the realm of faeries. To sleep under a hawthorn tree at Beltane was to gain entrance to the faerie realm. Hawthorn is associated with portals, doorways to magick realms, and the granting of wishes. Petitions written on ribbons and tied to the branches of the hawthorn would be carried by the wind to the faerie realm, where the denizens of magickal beings could choose to aid in human affairs. Hawthorn bark and berries are used in love spells.

Henbane

(Hyoscyamus niger)

History

Some of the earliest references to henbane are found in the Ebers papyrus, one of the earliest medical texts, where Egyptians describe henbane as "useful but dangerous." It is indigenous to northern Europe, with some varieties originating from the Mediterranean region, but it has spread west and is often found uncultivated near ancient ruins. It is associated with the priestesses of the oracle of Delphi and is thus considered a sacred herb.

Characteristics

Resembling the potato plant, henbane has grayish-green leaves that grow very close together. The texture of the leaves is both sticky and hairy. The flowers of henbane are yellow with curious violet veins. The aroma of the flowers is most often described as extremely unpleasant.

Magickal Properties

Henbane is a poisonous herb and should not be ingested or inhaled. When burned, it can induce a state of altered consciousness. In ancient witchcraft, henbane enabled witches to "fly on fire," a euphemism for a hallucination of flying when an ointment of henbane was applied to the skin. Today, henbane is used for divination and prophecy. It is only used with great caution, as an anodyne when a bundle is placed on an altar.

Hibiscus

(Hibiscus rosa-sinensis)

History
Hibiscus is native to the Far East and is believed to have originated in India or China. It was brought to Europe in the sixteenth century and is now cultivated throughout the world, where it is used in food and beverages.

Characteristics
Hibiscus is an annual herb bearing red flowers. It reaches a height of 4–5 feet. Hibiscus has culinary properties; the young flowers are used in sauces, jellies, jams, and elixirs. Infusions made from the blossoms are also consumed as a tea.

Magickal Properties
Used for invoking passion and in love magick, the colorful flowers of the hibiscus have a tart but pleasant taste. Hibiscus is also considered an offering of beauty and an acknowledgment of courage.

Honey secretion of Apis mellifera

History
Honey has been used as a remedy for so long, and though it is not an herb, it is an established part of folk medicine and herbal magick. Honey is frequently combined with herbs in oxymels and other preparations. Its high sugar content makes it resistant to bacteria. Jars of honey have been discovered in Egyptian tombs. They have not spoiled in 5,000 years.

Characteristics
Honey is a simple sugar made from the nectar of various flowers. It is an important nutrient and is widely used as a sweetener. It has a demulcent effect and soothes sore throats and eases cold symptoms.

The Modern Witchcraft Guide to Magickal Herbs

Magickal Properties

Honey is strongly associated with Aphrodite and as such plays an important role in love magick. Priestesses of Aphrodite and Demeter were known as the melissae, and were referred to as sacred bee priestesses. Honey is also used in candle magick. It creates a link between spells and witches.

Honeysuckle

(Lonicera caprifolium)

History

Honeysuckle was brought to the United States in the early nineteenth century and is considered an invasive plant. Its initial purpose was as an ornamental plant used to control soil erosion.

Characteristics

Honeysuckle is a night-blooming climbing shrub with long purplish-white or yellowish flowers and black berries. Known for its sweet nectar, honeysuckle is an evergreen plant native to Europe.

Magickal Properties

Honeysuckle has a sweet fragrance that makes it synonymous with affection. Used in love magick, honeysuckle blossoms represent deep fondness and warmth. It can be used to restore a waning love affair or to encourage a new love.

Hops

(Humulus lupulus)

History

Best known for its use in brewing ales and beer, hops has been used in Europe since the eleventh century. Its historic importance in brewing was mainly as a preservative and a preferred flavoring. Commercial cultivation in the United States began in Massachusetts in 1791.

Characteristics

Hops is a perennial plant that can grow back year after year if the root is left intact. The hops bines, or stems, can grow between 1½ and 2 feet. It is distinguished by its yellowish-green cones. Hops has many medicinal uses, including increasing appetite, increasing urination, and alleviating indigestion. It is also used to treat bladder infections and intestinal cramping.

Magickal Properties

Hops is used in trance magick and can be burned as incense to create a between-the-worlds state of consciousness, making it suitable for sabbat rituals as a burnt offering or as an altar offering.

Horehound

(Marrubium vulgare)

History

John Gerard made mention of horehound four hundred years ago in *Generall Historie of Plantes*, where he praised its efficacy as a tonic and a topical. Horehound has been used to treat all sorts of maladies from tuberculosis to asthma.

Characteristics

Part of the mint family, the leaves and flowering tops of the horehound herb have been used as folk medicine and in culinary craft. It is also used in cough drops and candy for its expectorant effects. It has a pleasant taste and an appealing fragrance.

Magickal Properties

Horehound is a stabilizing herb. It can be used for grounding rituals or to bring a witch back to center when things get intense. Horehound can also be used to amplify scrying. Place the dried flowers and leaves in a sachet and use it to charge and purify your crystals.

Horsetail

(Equisetum arvense)

History

The virtues of horsetail were referenced in "Songs of Labor," a poem by Quaker poet and abolitionist John Greenleaf Whittier in the 1800s. This "dull and flowerless weed" has been used in folk medicine as a topical in the treatment of wounds as well as a diuretic in the treatment of kidney and bladder issues.

Characteristics

Horsetail is a perennial plant that reproduces through spores, making it more closely related to ferns than to flowering herbs. Its stems are hollow like reeds. Also called "scouring rush," the stems of the horsetail contain silica, which can be used as a metal polish.

Magickal Properties

Horsetail has many magickal associations. Its reedlike structure makes it effective for invoking and honoring Pan, the horned god who represents wild nature. Horsetail's association with improving the appearance of metal connects it to love: Hephaestus won Aphrodite's heart by virtue of his skill with metalworking. Horsetail is useful in love magick of the passionate variety.

Hydrangea

(Hydrangea arborescens)

History

Hydrangea was used by the Cherokee as a diuretic and in the treatment of kidney stones. The Cherokee introduced the use of hydrangea to European settlers. In the 1900s, it was discovered that hydrangea contained a toxic substance in its early growth leaves. Despite its poisonous reputation, some people still chose to use hydrangea as an intoxicant, which would make them either euphoric or extremely ill.

Characteristics

Hydrangea is a shrub that grows along the eastern part of the United States and into the Midwest. It is best known and grown for its showy flowers; however, it has also been used in conventional medicine to treat infections of the urinary tract and bladder. Also called "seven barks," the hydrangea's root and rhizome were used by Native Americans as medicine.

Magickal Properties

Because of its beauty and its reputation as an herb with consciousness-altering properties, hydrangea makes a perfect altar offering, particularly in coven craft due to its attractive appearance. The altar is the stage upon which spiritual energies and the witch interact. Having hydrangea present on the altar accomplishes sympathetic magick, as the intention of spiritual communion is symbolized by the plant. Ornamental and spiritually significant, hydrangea serves as a conduit between the spirits of the land and the practitioners who honor them. Its attractive flowers are reminiscent of coven craft, as many individual flowers culminate in a powerful circle. Hydrangea can be placed on the altar during coven gatherings, then hung upside down and dried. Pinches of the dried flowers can be given to coven members in a sachet or pouch as an emblem of their belonging.

Hyssop

(Hyssopus officinalis)

History

Mentioned in the Bible in both the Old and New Testaments, the hyssop described is somewhat of a mystery and might refer to as many as eighteen different plants. However, hyssop has been proven effective as a remedy for coughs and colds.

Characteristics

Hyssop is a perennial shrub that grows along the roadsides in the United States. It is recognizable for its stalky clusters of bluish-purple flowers that resemble lavender. It is part of the mint family and is a common plant found in many a garden. Hyssop contains volatile oils that have a smell similar to camphor. It's often used as an infusion mixed with honey.

Magickal Properties

Hyssop is used in magick as a cleansing or clearing herb. It has been used on people, places, and objects to rid a person or space of unwanted and undesirable psychic energy. The diluted oil can be used for anointing doorways, altar tools, and ritual participants.

Jojoba

(Simmondsia chinensis)

History

For hundreds of years, Native Americans used the oil from the seeds of the jojoba plant as a hair tonic. The oil was absorbed into the scalp and imparted a silkiness to the hair while also improving the health of the scalp by reducing dandruff.

Characteristics

Jojoba is an evergreen shrub that produces a seed about the size of a peanut. The oil from this seed is ubiquitous in beauty products. It grows abundantly in rocky, dry areas in the Southwest including Arizona, California, and Mexico. When the seeds are expressed, they expel a wax that has similar physical properties as sperm oil: It remains liquid at room temperature, has a golden color, and combines easily with other oils.

Magickal Properties

The wax from jojoba seeds makes an excellent carrier oil for the dilution of essential oils. An important ingredient in aromatherapy, jojoba can also be used for clearing and banishing on its own.

Juniper

(Juniperus communis)

History
Widely used for over three hundred years, the berries from the juniper tree are used as a flavoring agent in gin. In folk medicine, juniper was used as a diuretic to treat kidney and bladder problems as well as indigestion and gas.

Characteristics
Juniper is an evergreen shrub with purplish, fleshy berries that are eaten or infused in a tea. Juniper is also an appetite stimulant and has culinary applications. It is often used as an ingredient in sauerkraut. Extract of the berries in alcohol is used both as a topical and as a spirit.

Magickal Properties
The magickal applications of juniper are numerous. The berries are potent protective charms and are known to increase psychic powers. Due to their attractive purple color, they are also associated with the crown chakra, representing spiritual attainment. Juniper is also a popular ingredient in incense.

Lady's Mantle

(Alchemilla vulgaris)

History
Native to Europe, lady's mantle has been observed growing as far north as the Arctic Circle. During the Middle Ages, lady's mantle was used in alchemy attempts to change base metals into gold. The "lady" in lady's mantle refers to the Queen of Heaven, the Virgin Mary. This is why it is written as possessive and not plural. Lady's mantle is also associated with the Egyptian goddess Sekhmet. The leaves of lady's mantle are thought to resemble the paw of a lion; hence, the herb is also known as

pied-de-lion in French and *leontopodium* in New Latin, from the Greek *leon* (lion) and *podion* (foot).

Characteristics

The broad green leaves of lady's mantle bear a resemblance to a cloak. The leaves and roots of lady's mantle have been used to treat maladies such as diarrhea, bloating, and menopausal symptoms, as well as inflammations. Root decoctions are used to treat ulcers, while tea made from the leaves is used as a gargle for sore throats.

Magickal Properties

Lady's mantle can be used psychically to invoke strength as well as concealment. Dew collected from the broad leaves is believed to be imbued with magickal powers. (The beads of dew were called "pearls that falleth in the night," and according to Culpeper, lady's mantle was a powerful aphrodisiac, imparting "lust to the worke of generacyon.")

Lavender
(Lavandula angustifolia)

History

Some common names for lavender, *Lavandula angustifolia*, include English lavender, French lavender, and true lavender. Some of the earliest recorded uses of lavender are by the Roman soldiers who used the wild-growing plant to perfume their bathwater and wash their clothes. Its name is derived from the Latin *lavare*, which translates as "to wash." Lavender is also associated with the element of air.

Characteristics

The evergreen leaves can have a bluish appearance and grow from 1 to 1¾ of an inch long. The flowers bloom on 1½–2½-inch spikes. Lavender requires full sun and excellent soil drainage in order to thrive. Its scent is relaxing and can be uplifting all at the same time. It can be placed in your pillow to help you sleep or mixed into essential oil for aromatherapy use.

Magickal Properties

Lavender is wonderful for use in edibles and elixirs, as well as spells and charms. Often called the "woman's herb," lavender is associated with spells related to calmness. Its purple blossoms resonate with the crown chakra, making this herb auspicious for spiritual attunement.

Lemon Balm

(Melissa officinalis)

History

Lemon balm has a long and storied use. From Dioscorides to Culpeper, as well as the pioneering herbalist Hildegard von Bingen, the many virtues of lemon balm have been recorded and celebrated. Some of these benefits include mood elevation and digestive issues, as well as toothaches.

Characteristics

A perennial herb, lemon balm is a member of the mint family. Its citrus-like fragrance and flavor make it a desirable herb for culinary applications as well as infusions and herbal teas. Native to the Mediterranean, lemon balm is cultivated throughout the world. It is also known as bee balm. Its leaves have a wrinkled appearance, and its flowers are tiny and white, sometimes appearing very pale yellow.

Magickal Properties

In magick, lemon balm is evocative of strong emotions. It is used in love magick to attract love and heal broken hearts. Since it is calming and soothing, it can be used in a ritual bath, consumed as an infusion, or used in a topical ointment.

Linden

(Tilia cordata)

History

Since the late Middle Ages, infusions of linden flowers have been used as a remedy for fever, headaches, indigestion, and hysteria.

Characteristics

These large deciduous trees, also called basswood, can grow up to 100 feet tall. Linden blooms in the spring, and its white and yellowish flowers are gathered soon after and dried thoroughly in the sun. (Linden flowers are delicate and spoil easily.) The flowers are very fragrant and are often used as a tea.

Magickal Properties

Linden flowers have nerve-calming properties. In magick, linden is used for calming, clearing, and de-stressing. For example, infusions of linden can be added to a ritual bath in preparation for a sabbat or rite.

Lobelia

(Lobelia inflata)

History

During the 1800s, lobelia was used in eclectic medicine and enjoyed a resurgence in popularity in the 1970s. Sometimes referred to as Indian tobacco, lobelia has been known to act as a stimulant with an effect similar to nicotine. Studies have shown that lobelia is not really safe to ingest or inhale, even though it has been used in some products meant to aid the cessation of smoking.

Characteristics

While lobelia is widely cultivated, it also grows wild in open woods and meadows in the eastern region of North America. Its small blue blossoms make it an attractive herb. Lobelia has branched stems, but its leaves and flowers are the parts used.

Magickal Properties

Lobelia is often used to clear a sacred space, in incense as an offering, or as part of a cleansing before a spell or rite; for example, to bless a space after a move. Lobelia promotes a general sense of well-being.

Lovage

(Levisticum officinale)

History

Legend holds that in the early Middle Ages, King Charlemagne was so enamored of the lovage plant that he had his castle gardens planted with stands of lovage. In the 1700s, infusions of lovage root combined with other herbs were used as a folk remedy for the treatment of inflammations. It is also known as the Maggi plant because of its association with magick, both in love magick and protective magick, and is widely cultivated throughout the United States and Europe because of its flavor.

Characteristics

Lovage is a tall perennial herb with culinary and medicinal applications. It has dark green leaves that are often used as a seasoning for meats, soups, and stews.

Magickal Properties

Lovage root and leaves are used in love magick and to invoke good fortune. The root can be dried and ground into a powder and added to charms designed to attract a love interest. Superstition leads many to believe that it is more effective on men.

Marshmallow

(Althaea officinalis)

History

Marshmallow has been used both as a remedy and as a food source since ancient times. Marshmallow is referenced by Pliny the Elder, who touted its healing efficacy: "Whosoever shall take a spoonful of the mallows shall that day be free from all diseases that may come to him." Arabic physicians used a poultice made from the leaves to treat inflammations. The genus name comes from the Greek word *althainein*, meaning "to heal," which indicates marshmallow as a healing herb.

Characteristics

Marshmallow grows well in moist and sandy soil, reaching heights of 2–5 feet and requires full sunlight. It is a gelatinous herb and has a slimy consistency. Its uses range from laxatives to lotions to soothing skin irritations, and it can even be used as a toothpaste.

Magickal Properties

Marshmallow is used in handfastings and sex magick. It is considered an aphrodisiac and has the ability to inspire fidelity in a mate. It is also used in cleansing rituals and for protection.

Milk Thistle

(Silybum marianum)

History

Native to the Mediterranean region, milk thistle was originally found during ancient times in areas from North Africa through the Middle East, making it a Hellenic herb. Pliny the Elder refers to milk thistle as an ingredient in a tonic that soothes and heals the liver, recommending the juice of the milk thistle mixed with honey as a treatment for "carrying off bile." It is also considered to increase lactation. It is identified by its green leaves that are mottled with white. Milk thistle has a connection to Mary the Mother of God in the Catholic faith. Christian lore holds that while nursing the infant god, milk cascaded from Mary's breast onto the milk thistle plant, thus imbuing it with sacred powers. Because of this, milk thistle is also referred to as "Our Lady's Thistle" and "Mary's Thistle."

Characteristics

Milk thistle is characterized by its slender stalks, prickly leaves, and distinctive purple flowers that emanate from a round, green base with spiny protrusions. The feathery purple petals have white veins. Extracts from milk thistle seeds are used for medicinal purposes.

Magickal Properties

In magick, it is used for protection, purification, bestowing blessings, and breaking hexes. Placing a bowl full of milk thistle in a room will improve the energy of the environment. Stuffing a charm or poppet with milk thistle is a way to counteract a hex.

Mistletoe
(Phoradendron leucarpum)

History
Because mistletoe bloomed in wintertime, it was regarded as a sacred herb by the ancient druids. In 1820, Washington Irving included a reference to kissing under the mistletoe as a part of the English Christmas tradition in one of his essays, along with gathering around a Yule log. This helped the practice of kissing under the mistletoe gain popularity in the United States.

Characteristics
Mistletoe is a parasitic epiphyte: a plant that grows only upon other plants. There are many different types of mistletoe. The berries are poisonous, but the leaves have been used in folk medicine for everything from anxiety to cancer. Different types of mistletoe have very different effects. Mistletoe is characterized by its waxy, white berries and its small evergreen leaves, which range in color from pale yellow to dark green.

Magickal Properties
Mistletoe is a calming herb and promotes feelings of warmth. Because of its role in Yuletide decor, it is considered a love magick charm. It is also associated with fertility.

Mugwort
(Artemisia vulgaris)

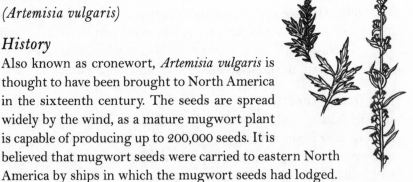

History
Also known as cronewort, *Artemisia vulgaris* is thought to have been brought to North America in the sixteenth century. The seeds are spread widely by the wind, as a mature mugwort plant is capable of producing up to 200,000 seeds. It is believed that mugwort seeds were carried to eastern North America by ships in which the mugwort seeds had lodged.

Characteristics

Mugwort is distinct because of its fingerlike dark green leaves that display a silvery, almost woolen, texture on the underside. A perennial plant, mugwort has a dense and expansive but shallow root system. New shoots will burst through the earth in early spring, and flowering culminates from July through September.

Magickal Properties

Named for the Greek goddess Artemis, the maiden goddess of the hunt, the silvery leaves of mugwort have proved to be a potent source of magick and healing. Mugwort grows in profuse proliferation and reminds us of our wild nature as well as our connection to the moon. Mugwort is known to awaken the psychic eye, aid dream work, and alleviate menstrual discomfort.

Mullein

(Verbascum thapsus)

History

Referenced by Dioscorides in the first century C.E., mullein has been widely used in folk medicine as a remedy for coughs and colds and was also featured in the *National Formulary*, one of the two compendia that made up the *United States Pharmacopeia* (which was published annually up until 1936). Native to Europe, the plant is believed to have been introduced to the United States by early colonists.

Characteristics

This biennial herb has a wooly texture and large leaves that form a rosette pattern in their first year. In the second year of growth, mullein develops its tall stem, which can reach 4 feet or more in height. The stem culminates with a profusion of yellow flowers. The leaves and flowers are used.

Magickal Properties

Mullein is used for invoking peace and restoring relationships. If you wish to mend a rift, right a wrong, or heal using mullein in spells and charms, include some of the herb with a rose quartz and a copper coin (such as a penny) in a sachet or pouch and either deliver it to the involved parties or leave the charm in the place where the disagreement unfolded.

Myrrh

(Commiphora myrrha)

History
Used in trade since biblical times, myrrh was valued for its fragrance and also as an embalming agent. In folk medicine, myrrh has been used as an antiseptic, an astringent, and as an emmenagogue (a treatment to stimulate menstruation).

Characteristics
Valued for its fragrance, myrrh is a gummy resin obtained from cuts in the bark of small trees in the *Commiphora* genus. The yellow and brown secretions are small and pebble-like, often having a tear-shaped appearance. Myrrh is native to Ethiopia, Somalia, and the Arabian Peninsula.

Magickal Properties
Myrrh is sacred to the dead. It is a popular ingredient in incense and is a powerful offering on its own. It is also a cleansing herb. Burning myrrh on a circle of charcoal is an effective way to cleanse a large space in order to prepare for ritual or spellcraft.

Oatstraw

(Avena sativa)

History
Avena sativa is native to the Mediterranean region, and its use dates back to the medieval era, when it was used to support brain health. Today, it is commonly used as feed for livestock.

Characteristics
Oatstraw is an annual grass, hardy and able to survive in a variety of soil conditions. It can reach a height of 5 feet and grows in cool, temperate regions. It is the same plant that produces oats used for oatmeal, but oatstraw is harvested while the seeds are still green and includes the grassy green husks.

Magickal Properties

Oatstraw is a calming herb with nerve-calming properties. As such, it is used to reduce anxiety. Because it can cause a sense of well-being and relaxation, oatstraw is associated with the lowering of inhibitions, making it important in love magick. "Sowing your wild oats" is a euphemism for promiscuous behavior. Although it is calming, it is not a sedative; rather, it energizes, making it an effective aphrodisiac. Oatstraw is also nourishing to the skin and can be used as a base for beauty magick.

Parsley

(Petroselinum crispum)

History

Parsley has been in use for more than two thousand years. The Cherokee used it as a tonic to alleviate bladder problems. Parsley was also used as a funerary herb in ancient Greece. Wreaths of parsley adorned the tombs of the dead. Medicinally, the taproot, seeds, and leaves were used.

Characteristics

Parsley is a popular biennial culinary herb with divided leaves and clusters of yellow flowers. Parsley can grow up to 3 feet tall by its second year and is slow to germinate. It is ubiquitous as a garnish as well as a flavoring.

Magickal Properties

Parsley is strongly associated with death. It is sacred to Persephone, and legend states that the lengthy germination period for parsley to grow is due to the seeds needing to travel to the underworld and then back again before establishing their long taproot. Parsley is used as a garnish because ancient custom holds that an offering to the dead must be made in order to show gratitude for the lives sacrificed for the meal. In keeping with these ancient practices, modern witches can use parsley to decorate the Samhain altar, either with wreaths or bundles of the fresh herb.

Passionflower

(Passiflora incarnata)

History
Although this plant was not known during biblical times, it has been attributed with symbols of the crucifixion of Christ dating back to the early 1600s. The unique blossom is said to represent the crown of thorns and the hammer and nails, as well as the loyal apostles. Because the flowers have five petals and five sepals, this is believed to represent ten of the twelve apostles. Peter and Judas are excluded because Peter denied Christ and Judas betrayed him. Passionflower was discovered by Spanish explorers who encountered the herb in Peru. It was included in the *National Formulary* during the early twentieth century due to its reputation for producing a calming effect. It has even been included in chewing gum.

Characteristics
Passionflower is a perennial climbing vine. The exotic-looking flowers only stay open for around one day. Passionflowers need full sun to partial shade and moist, well-drained soil with mulch on top. Because they climb, passionflowers require some kind of armature upon which to grow. Passionflowers are also heavy feeders, so adding compost to the soil composition is a must.

Magickal Properties
Passionflower is a calming herb, so it can uplift the spirit and represents gentleness. When planted near the home, passionflower brings peace. Because it is a clinging vine, it is also used in love magick for drawing and maintaining affection.

Peppermint

(Mentha x piperita)

History
In 1696, a hybrid of spearmint sprouted in a field in England, giving us one of the most popular and widely used herbs since. Its first appearance in the

London Pharmacopoeia was in 1721; however, it was purportedly used by ancient Egyptians as a treatment for upset stomachs.

Characteristics

Peppermint is very difficult to grow from seed and does not breed true; therefore, it is mainly propagated through cuttings—plants sprouted from seeds will not necessarily be identical to the parent plant, but plants propagated by cuttings will. Growing up to 3 feet in height, peppermint does not tolerate dry conditions and grows best in proximity to ponds and streams. It has a tendency to spread, and the plants like to be moved every few years. Peppermint contains menthol, which differentiates it from spearmint. It is used as a digestive aid as well as a flavoring herb. It is a common ingredient in gum, toothpaste, and tea.

Magickal Properties

Mint is always used in spells for money, luck, and general good fortune. Growing peppermint in the home is believed to bring good luck and protection. It is also associated with healing and purification.

Pine

(Pinus)

History

Native to the southern Atlantic coastline, pine is famed for its beauty, strength, and fragrance, as well as its importance to the lumber industry. Pine was among the most sought-after species of trees in the late eighteenth century and was a major export of New England.

Characteristics

Pine is a conifer with aromatic needles that grow in spirals. Growing throughout the southeastern United States, pine prefers dry, sandy soil. Pines reproduce via their seed-bearing cones.

Magickal Properties

To pine for someone is to long for them almost to the point of pain. As such, pine is a powerful ingredient in love spells. The cones can be used as an herbal talisman and make a beautiful and aromatic addition to potpourri blends.

Red Clover

(Trifolium pratense)

History

Red clover is mentioned by Pliny the Elder as well as John Gerard. Although descriptions of its therapeutic value have changed over the years, it was recommended for the treatment of everything from syphilis to psoriasis and from eczema to anxiety in the early nineteenth century. Because of the shape of its leaves, it is associated with divinity. The three lobes of the leaf join together at a common point, representing the trinity of maiden, mother, and crone or father, son, and spirit.

Characteristics

Red clover is considered a woman's herb. It is often cited as a remedy used to ease some of the natural effects of menopause such as hot flashes and breast tenderness. A perennial herb, red clover can grow up to 16 inches. Its pinkish-purple flowers bloom from late spring to early fall. It grows profusely in the wild and is commonly foraged.

Magickal Properties

Red clover is used for purification. An infusion of red clover can be used to cleanse ritual tools and ritual space. Making a red clover tea and letting it cool, then transferring it to a spray bottle can be an effective way to disperse its cleansing properties. It represents the crone aspect of the triple goddess.

Red Raspberry

(Rubus idaeus)

History

Raspberries are believed to have been used since the first century. The Roman agriculturist Palladius mentions the discovery of raspberry seeds in the fourth century. During the medieval era, only the wealthy had the pleasure of consuming raspberries. Commercial cultivation of raspberries is said to have begun in western Europe in the seventeenth century.

Characteristics

Described as native to Europe but also believed to have originated in Asia, raspberry is widely cultivated. The leaves are used in poultices and teas. It is an astringent herb and is used as a women's tonic, credited with easing menstrual discomfort and alleviating morning sickness in pregnancy. While the fruit is often used for food, it is the leaves that are prized for their therapeutic value. Relatively easy to grow, raspberries do well in both cool and warm climates and require full sun. The fruits arrive in summer.

Magickal Properties

Because of their beneficial association with women, raspberries are used in fertility charms and love magick. You can make a simple love potion by soaking the berries in wine. For invocations for fertility, an infusion of the leaves may be consumed. Because the berries are loaded with seeds, they can also be dried and included in fertility charms.

Rhodiola

(Rhodiola rosea)

History

Rhodiola has been used for hundreds of years. First mentioned by Dioscorides, the root has been used to treat a variety of ailments, such as anxiety and fatigue. Originally referred to as *rodia riza* in the first century, the herb was renamed by the Swiss taxonomist Carolus Linnaeus in the 1900s. A cluster of greenish-yellow flowers culminates at the top of rhodiola's sturdy stalk.

Characteristics

Rhodiola is a perennial flowering herb and is considered an adaptogen, helping the body to adjust to stress. It is also known as arctic root and golden root. When cut, the stem has a fragrance similar to a rose. It has been used in a similar fashion to ginseng and is usually prepared as an infusion.

Magickal Properties

Rhodiola is used in magick to amplify energy. Including the root in a charm can increase its power. Rhodiola root can also function as an herbal talisman for courage and strength. It is also used in love magick for invoking fertility and virility. Using the flowers and stems in a flower water can be used to consecrate a sexy space. Heat distilled water and immerse the flowers and cut stems in the heated water. Allow the herb to steep for several hours, then transfer the liquid into a spray bottle. Add a tablespoon of witch hazel or grain alcohol as a preservative; otherwise keep the potion refrigerated.

Rose
(Rosa gallica)

History
The French rose is one of the oldest cultivated garden plants. Also called "apothecary rose," the open blossoms occur in an almost limitless array of varieties. Roses are believed to have been first cultivated in China, with a history rumored to date back five thousand years.

Characteristics
The rose is a hermaphroditic deciduous shrub that grows up to 6 feet tall. It flowers from early to midsummer and does well in light woodlands with partial shade to full sun. Roses require moist soil. Its petals are edible and can be eaten raw or cooked. Rose petals are used in teas, spice blends, and in rose water, which is an ingredient in Turkish delight, a popular confection.

Magickal Properties
There is perhaps no other flower as strongly associated with romance as the rose. Known as the queen of flowers, the gift of a rose has long been held as a gesture of love. Roses are used in magick to evoke sexual attraction. The rose has correlations with spiritual enlightenment because sacred tools and traditions, such as the rosary and the esoteric Rosicrucian occult society, bear its name.

Rosehip

(Rosa canina and rugosa, acicularis,
cinnamomea)

History
Rosehips were prized as a source of vitamin
C and as such were used medicinally during
World War II as an alternative to citrus.

Characteristics
Rosehips are the small, red, oblong fruit typi-
cally of the dog rose and the Japanese rose. Used in capsules, extracts,
teas, and purées, rosehips are consumed mainly for their high vitamin
C content. They are also used in jellies and syrups. Roses grow to a
height of 5 feet and bear their fruit after the blossom has faded.

Magickal Properties
Rosehips are used in the pursuit of both peace and love. The dried
fruits can be strung on a thread and worn as a magickal herbal talisman to attract love and affection as well as serenity.

Rosemary

(Rosmarinus officinalis)

History
In French antiquity, rosemary was also referred
to as *incensier* because it was often used as incense. Rosemary was sacred to the Spanish, who
cited rosemary as being associated with the Virgin
Mother, who sought shelter under its branches.

Characteristics
With its aromatic, needlelike leaves, the rosemary plant grows in a
bush and can become quite large under the right growing conditions.
It is used extensively in culinary, medicinal, and magickal applications. It is popular as a savory ingredient in cooking as well as healing. Its diuretic properties reduce puffiness from fluid retention. It is
also an effective hair tonic, particularly for those with dark hair.

Magickal Properties

Rosemary is strongly associated with fidelity and memory, as Shakespeare notably referenced the herb in *Hamlet*. Ophelia, recalling her deceased father, produces a sprig of rosemary for "remembrance," solidifying the herb's association with storytellers and lovers—those who particularly wish to be remembered. Rosemary can be bundled in smudge sticks and burned as incense, added to seasonal dishes and eaten, or crushed in a mortar and pestle and added to sachets and charms.

Rue

(Ruta graveolens)

History

In pre-Christian times, rue was grown around temples and was considered sacred in ancient Rome. Rue was called "herb of grace" by early Christians, who apparently used it as a ward against witches. Because of this association, rue was also known as witchbane.

Characteristics

Rue is a perennial shrub native to southern Europe. It has yellow flowers and a musky scent that many consider to be unpleasant. The leaves are bluish-green in color. One of the oldest garden plants, rue can grow almost anywhere.

Magickal Properties

Rue is used as a protective charm. For example, a bundle of rue hung over a doorway served as a ward against evil spirits. It is also associated with enhancing creativity as well as psychic abilities.

Saffron

(Crocus sativus)

History

As early as the sixth century, saffron was used as an aphrodisiac, a stimulant, and a means of spiritual enhancement. A fifteenth-century imam described saffron as the scent of the seventh heaven, which is why saffron is likened to the highest level of spiritual attainment as the embodiment of paradise.

Characteristics

Saffron is only about 6 inches tall and flowers in the autumn. Its leaves are long and usually blue or purple and wrap themselves around the three stigmas. Saffron grown from seed will take three years to flower and requires a sheltered environment with sandy soil that drains well.

Magickal Properties

Revered as a celestial plant due to its color, saffron is highly associated with heaven and gold. Its perfume is said to be the scent of heaven, giving saffron angelic properties. Saffron's association with angels can be used in magick to protect, guard, and ward off evil. Saffron powder can be sprinkled on a hot coal and burned as incense when invoking angelic energy.

Sage

(Salvia officinalis)

History

Sage is native to the Mediterranean region, and its use has been documented by Dioscorides as a topical as well as medicinal tea. It was used by ancient Romans as a digestive aid and as a fertility aid by the Egyptians. In classical Greek society, sage was used as a preservative and for memory enhancement. From the first millennium, sage has been cultivated with intention. Its name means "salvation."

Characteristics

Sage is a well-known and beloved garden plant. A member of the mint family, sage is characterized by its fuzzy leaves and flowers that range from blue to white, and, more infrequently, purplish pink. It has been used extensively as a remedy and is cultivated in the temperate zones of North America and Europe. A perennial evergreen shrub, sage is used as a healing herb, a culinary herb, and a magickal herb.

Magickal Properties

Sage is used for cleansing magickal tools and spaces. It is useful for invoking spiritual purity and for grounding and centering before any magickal endeavor. Varieties of sage have been dried and combined with other herbs such as cedar or sweetgrass and used by indigenous Americans in the sacred smudging ceremony for hundreds of years. This practice has been widely adopted by many neo-pagan practitioners and witches. Sage is also used by modern witches in fertility magick and for invoking luck and prosperity.

Savory
(Satureja hortensis)

History

Ancient herbals frequently mention two varieties of savory: summer and winter. Highly aromatic, savory is mentioned by the poet Virgil, who advocated for the planting of savory near beehives in order for the flavor to be imparted to the honey. It was used by ancient Romans as a substitute for salt. Its cultivation was prohibited during the Middle Ages due to its reputation as an aphrodisiac.

Characteristics

Also called summer savory, *Satureja hortensis* is an aromatic member of the mint family. Savory is highly valued as a spice, prized for its delicious peppery flavor. It is an annual plant (unlike *Satureja montana*, or winter savory, which is a perennial) and a carminative herb used as an appetite stimulant and as an astringent. Relatively easy to grow, savory has thin, dark green leaves and small white or pinkish-purple flowers. It achieves a height of 18 inches and enjoys full sun and compost in the soil mix.

Magickal Properties

Summer savory is used in sex magick as an aphrodisiac. It can be added to food in order to increase desire. It is also used for fertility spells. The leaves can be steeped and the infusion consumed as a love potion, and the seeds can be used in an herbal talisman.

Skullcap

(Scutellaria lateriflora)

History

First introduced into American medicine by a doctor named Lawrence Van Derveer in 1773, skullcap was introduced in the *United States Pharmacopeia* in 1863 and continued to be recommended for use until 1916. Skullcap was used in the treatment of hydrophobia and as a calming tonic.

Characteristics

Skullcap is part of the mint family. It grows up to 4 feet tall and has very small, colorful flowers that span the spectrum from purplish blue to pink and white. The stems, leaves, and flowers are generally used in a tincture.

Magickal Properties

Skullcap is associated with fidelity. It is also used as an herb to attract money. Placing some skullcap in a dish and putting coins on top is a spell to invoke wealth. Skullcap used in love magick is believed to promote loyalty and faithfulness.

Seneca Snakeroot

(Polygala senega)

History
Used by Native Americans as a remedy, Seneca snakeroot was originally believed to cure snake bites as well as coughs and colds. It was also used for toothaches and earaches.

Characteristics
Seneca snakeroot is a perennial herb that blooms with small, white flowers. It grows in the eastern region of North America from southern Canada to South Carolina. It gets its name from the twisted appearance of its yellowish-brown root. Its aroma and taste are similar to wintergreen, and it is often used to treat coughs.

Magickal Properties
Snakeroot is a banishing herb used for dispelling unwanted energy. You can make a cleansing oil by adding snakeroot to a jar and covering it with olive oil. Let the root steep in the oil for 6 weeks and then use the infusion to anoint doorways, surfaces, and other aspects of the environment that require an energetic adjustment. (Olive oil is sacred to the goddess Athena. She is a goddess of wisdom but also of strategy. She depicts the gorgon on her aegis, or shield, and is thus associated with snake energy.) Just as the snake sheds its skin, using snakeroot for banishing is a great way to release old patterns before invoking the new.

St. John's Wort

(Hypericum perforatum)

History
St. John's wort is one of the oldest-known remedies and was widely used from the time of Dioscorides through the Middle Ages and is still cited as useful in the treatment of anxiety today. Its use dates back to the first century, as it was used by a military doctor by the name of Proscurides. Magickally, it was used as an apotropaic against disease, demons, and witches, who were greatly feared during the Middle Ages.

Characteristics

St. John's wort is a woody shrub with bright yellow star-shaped flowers. It can grow up to 3 feet tall and 2 feet wide and requires well-drained soil and full sun or partial shade. It is a relatively hardy plant and can tolerate a range of soil conditions, except very alkaline.

Magickal Properties

Because of its cheerful color and the fact that it blooms very close to the summer solstice, St. John's wort is used magickally to invoke the solar energies of the god principle, the embodiment of masculine energy that manifests as the consort and balance to the divine feminine. Solar deities such as Apollo, Belenos, and Lugh can be represented on the Litha altar with boughs of St. John's wort. Additionally, St. John's wort can be used to promote calmness and peace. It is also used in faerie magick. By touching the correct number of blossoms to a faerie stone, the portal to the faerie realm is said to be revealed.

Stinging Nettle
(Urtica dioica)

History

Nettle was used in ancient Rome in a curious manner. During the advent of the Roman Empire, soldiers would find themselves far from the warmth of their native Mediterranean land and, being unaccustomed to colder climates, would use nettle as a way to warm themselves by gathering bundles of nettle leaves and hitting themselves with it. This process is known as urtication, named for the stinging nettle plant, and is still used as a folk remedy. Considered sacred to the Norse god of thunder, Thor, stinging nettle was used for protection against lightning by throwing a bundle of nettle onto a fire.

Characteristics

Stinging nettle has tiny hairs that cover the leaf and stem. These hairs are hollow and filled with venom. When a sentient being passes by the stinging nettle and brushes against it, the histamine is released, causing irritation. The dried leaves are void of histamine and do not sting. Likewise, stewing the leaves of the stinging nettle will also cause it to lose its sting, making it an effective remedy for inflammation such as arthritis.

Magickal Properties

When sewn into a sachet or carried in a pouch, stinging nettle will amplify courage. It is also used to increase virility.

Tansy

(Tanacetum vulgare)

History

Tansy has a long history of use in folk medicine as an anthelmintic herb to destroy parasites. Because it contains the toxic compound thujone, it is not recommended for consumption in large quantities. Ask an herbal practitioner before using.

Characteristics

Tansy is strongly aromatic and is characterized by its bright yellow flowers. It grows up to 3 feet, and although it is native to Europe, it is widely cultivated in the United States. The dried leaves and flowers are generally used in infusions as well as a culinary herb. It is used to flavor cakes and other sweets during the rites of spring.

Magickal Properties

Tansy is a magickally powerful herb effective for banishing spells. If you want someone or something out of your life, take a photograph or symbol of that person or situation and place it on a black cloth on your altar. Cover it with tansy flowers and allow the flowers to wilt. When the flowers have dried, you can crush them and burn them on a charcoal, along with a representation or effigy of the person or situation that you need to banish.

Tea Tree

(Melaleuca alternifolia)

History

While the tea tree plant has no relation to the *sinensis* that yields black, white, and green tea, this herb gets its name from the infusion made by the sailors of the crew of Captain James Cook in 1770, when they dropped anchor off the coast of New South Wales and discovered this aromatic herb growing in the swamp. It was later discovered that tea tree had been used by the indigenous people as a topical antiseptic. During World War II, tea tree oil was used to lubricate machinery in munition factories as a method of decreasing infections among the workers injured by said machinery.

Characteristics

Tea tree is most often used as a distilled oil obtained by steaming the leaves. It is a powerful antiseptic and is used to treat fungal infections and repel insects. Its volatile oil is always diluted when used as a topical, otherwise it has the power to destroy skin.

Magickal Properties

Tea tree is a powerful healer. It is also a very effective protective herb. Placing a mirror on your windowsill and charging it with a drop of tea tree oil is an effective protective charm. Bundles of leaves can also be used to protect a space when they are hung about a dwelling or room.

Thorn Apple

(Datura stramonium)

History

The thorn apple originates from the region of the Black Sea and the Caspian Sea. It was most likely spread by animals due to its spiny and sticky seed pods that easily lodge in fur. Thorn apple does not appear to have been known prior to the Renaissance. Thorn apple was brought to America by colonists so early on that some botanists thought it was a native plant.

Characteristics

Thorn apple is an annual plant that requires full sun and protection from wind. It is easy to cultivate and easy to recognize. Thorn apple has white flowers shaped like funnels, and its fruit or "apples" are about the size of a walnut and are covered in spines.

Magickal Properties

Thorn apple is associated with the worshippers of both Kali and Dionysus, adding to its mystery and danger. Used in sorcery and love magick, thorn apple is also among the ingredients in the witch's flying ointment.

Thyme
(Thymus vulgaris)

History

Thyme has been used for thousands of years. The flowers and leaves have been cited as a remedy for stomach ailments and respiratory problems. Historically, thyme was used in the embalming process and as a ward against the black death.

Characteristics

Thyme is a perennial evergreen herb that is part of the mint family. Native to the Mediterranean, thyme contains thymol, which is a naturally occurring biocide. Thymol (a phytochemical extracted from thyme) is used in mouthwashes such as Listerine because it stops bacteria from growing. The herb itself is safe to consume, and the phytochemical is only toxic in very large amounts only when ingested. (That's why we spit out the mouthwash.) Thyme is a renowned culinary spice with medicinal properties as well as ornamental appeal. Its gray-green leaves, tiny flowers, and pungent aroma make it highly desirable.

Magickal Properties

Thyme is a symbol of bravery, love, and attraction. It is also used in protective magick and is sacred to the dead. When burned as an incense, thyme brings courage. It is also associated with the faerie realm. Drinking an infusion of thyme at Litha would enable the practitioner to observe the dance of the sídhe.

Valerian

(Valeriana officinalis)

History
Valerian has been used for over a thousand years as a calming agent. Due to the strong odor of its root, valerian is rumored to have been what the Pied Piper used to rid Hamelin of its rats, as its pungent odor is said to be attractive to rats.

Characteristics
Valerian is a tall perennial herb with a hollow stem and either white or reddish flowers. It is also referred to as garden heliotrope. The rhizome and root hairs are harvested in the fall in the plant's second year of growth.

Magickal Properties
Valerian is an effective banishing herb. The dried root can be used to dispel unwanted energy. It is also used in dream work, as ingesting valerian is believed to produce a highly relaxed state. Due to its odor, it is not usually prepared as an infusion; rather, the ground-up root is consumed directly, often in the form of capsules.

Verbena

(Verbena officinalis)

History
Used since the medieval era, verbena, also known as vervain, is considered an ancient healing plant. It is also called "herb of grace," or *herba sacra*. The flowering heads and leaves were used to address ailments including kidney and bladder issues as well as menstrual cramps.

Characteristics
Verbena, or vervain, is delicate and slender with pale lilac-colored flower clusters that culminate at the top of a leafless stem. A perennial herb, vervain is native to the Mediterranean but is cultivated

throughout Asia and Europe. The aerial, or aboveground, parts of the herb are used.

Magickal Properties

Verbena is used as an altar adornment and as a sacred herbal tool. Verbena is symbolic of nurturing. It is a mother's herb. It is also used ritually in adorning walking sticks used to "beat the bounds" or bless and protect the perimeter of a property.

Violet

(Viola odorata)

History

Violets have been cultivated for over two thousand years. In ancient classical mythology, the daughter of the goddess Demeter, Persephone, was gathering violets when she was abducted into the underworld. The word "violet" has its roots in *ion*, the Greek word for "violet," which is derived from one of the mistresses of Zeus.

Characteristics

Violets are prized for their color, fragrance, and culinary and medicinal uses. Violets should be planted in either early spring or late August so that they can establish roots before the intense heat of summer or the freeze of winter. They prefer cool, damp places. They bloom from April to May and then again in the late fall. Violets are used as a remedy for headaches, constipation, coughs, and as a topical for nourishing the skin.

Magickal Properties

Violets are associated with love and dreams. To invoke prophetic dreams that will reveal the object of your passion, sleep with a sachet of violets under your pillow. You can also make a prophetic violet potion by infusing one or two handfuls of the leaves in a steaming pot. Add some honey and drink before dreaming. Take note of the visions that the violets impart. They will reveal the longings of your heart.

Witch Hazel
(Hamamelis virginiana)

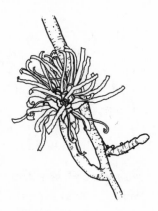

History
Introduced to early settlers by Native Americans, witch hazel is indigenous to the United States and was used as a topical for the reduction of inflammation.

Characteristics
Witch hazel is a late bloomer, showing its bright yellow, threadlike flowers in the late fall, past the time when other plants have shed their leaves. The leaves and bark are used as a poultice and in steam distillations of the aerial parts of the plant.

Magickal Properties
Used for wands, dowsing, and other tools of divination, witch hazel factors heavily into magick. It is a protective herb, and its distillation is frequently used in aromatherapy sprays as a preservative. Witch hazel is also associated with inspiration and love.

Wormwood
(Artemisia absinthium)

History
The earliest reference to wormwood is in the Ebers papyrus, which was obtained in 1873 by the Egyptologist George Ebers. The Ebers papyrus is believed to have been written in 3500 B.C.E. Part of the *Artemisia* family, wormwood was used as a flavoring agent in an alcoholic drink that was popular in the late eighteenth century in Paris. Known as absinthe, wormwood was considered a dangerous poison mainly because of the outrageous actions of those who consumed it. By 1915, it was banned. It is considered a mind-altering substance.

Characteristics

Native to Europe, wormwood has a pleasant if musty aroma, a bitter taste, and a sinister reputation. It is a slow-growing deciduous shrubby perennial plant and is common in the United States. Wormwood has deep roots, silvery hairy leaves, and intensely yellow flowers. It can propagate itself reasonably well and likes to grow near the sea. It reaches a height of about 18 inches.

Magickal Properties

Wormwood is a powerful apotropaic herb, which means that it protects from evil. Legend holds that wormwood planted around a garden will keep pests and snakes away. Wormwood is used for boundary magick. When you need to establish a protective distance from a person or situation, adding wormwood to your spells and charms will help keep undesirable people and energy away while serving as a protective charm as well. It is especially effective when used in the dual function of banishing and protecting. It can also be burned at the beginning of a ritual during circle casting.

Yarrow

(Achillea millefolium)

History

Yarrow is a famed healing herb, used for centuries in northern and western Europe and by the Native American people as well. Yarrow was also described in Chinese culture in place of coins in the popular oracle known as the I Ching. Legends state that the warrior Achilles was bathed in a yarrow infusion, which gave him protection in battle. The famed hero would then carry yarrow with him into battle in order to treat wounded soldiers. European colonists are said to have brought yarrow with them across the Atlantic, whereupon it was introduced to the Native Americans, who used a tea made from yarrow as a treatment for menorrhea.

Characteristics

Yarrow is characterized by its white flowers that bloom atop straight stalks with grayish-green serrated leaves that have a feathery appearance. It is used to treat nosebleeds and other wounds. Yarrow tea has been used as a fever reducer.

Magickal Properties

Yarrow is used for divination and spellwork. Its prophetic powers have been cited in predicting the outcome of romantic couplings.

Yellow Dock
(Rumex crispus)

History

Yellow dock root has been recommended by herbalists for hundreds of years. It has served as both a food source and a remedy.

Characteristics

A perennial herb, yellow dock has a deep yellow root that can reach a depth of 5 feet. Yellow dock has been used in remedies for constipation. Its green leaves are eaten but only in small quantities, as they are known to block calcium absorption. The root is considered anti-inflammatory and is used to soothe irritations of the nasal passages.

Magickal Properties

Yellow dock is used for purification. As an herbal talisman, it is also used in prosperity magick. The ground-up herb is said to attract customers when sprinkled around a place of business.

Yohimbe

(Pausinystalia yohimbe)

History
Discovered by German missionaries, yohimbe was brought back to Europe and marketed as a sexual stimulant. In western Africa, it was used as a remedy for fevers and leprosy.

Characteristics
Native to Africa, yohimbe is an evergreen tree that can grow up to 90 feet tall. It grows in parts of Nigeria, Cameroon, and the Democratic Republic of the Congo. It dilates the blood vessels of the skin and mucous membranes, the effect of which is the lowering of blood pressure. It is generally not considered safe to ingest, and yet it is still sold as a drug. (Self-administration of an herb that is known to lower blood pressure is not recommended.) One description of its recommended use calls for a decoction of the bark, then straining and sweetening the beverage.

Magickal Properties
Yohimbe is best known as an aphrodisiac with a reputation for igniting desire. The bark is used in love magick. It is not necessary to consume the bark, as it can be used in herbal charms or as an ingredient in incense.

PART III

HOW TO USE HERBS IN MAGICK

Now that you have had a primer on the origins of Western herbalism, learned how to grow and cultivate these herbs, and familiarized yourself with culinary and healing properties of herbs that you will encounter, it is time to dig deep and apply your knowledge to spellcraft. In this part, we will depart from the earthly realms and use herbs for magickal applications in everything from beauty spells to aphrodisiacs, divination and oracles, as well as ritual and altar craft.

Chapter 5

BOTANICALS AND BEAUTY: HERBAL SPELLS AND CHARMS TO MAKE YOU GLOW

Cultivating beauty on your own terms can be viewed as a radical act. Women are bombarded with overly sexualized images of femininity on a daily basis, and by redefining beauty, witches can reclaim an empowering and necessary sense of identity. For far too long, standards of beauty have been dictated by societal pressure and not personal preference. In pop culture, witches are often portrayed as ugly because we are misunderstood, and we are feared because of our power and our potential to effect change.

Think of herbal beauty magick as a reclaiming of what it means to be beautiful. Attractiveness is a powerful quality. It doesn't refer to an outward visage as much as it defines your ability to attract what you want and to manifest your desires. Herbal preparations can be made to address a host of beauty issues, both internal and external. In this chapter, you will learn how to create your own herbal- and magick-infused salves, creams, and perfumes.

CELEBRATING MAGICKAL BEAUTY

When you create your own beauty routines, infuse them with herbs, and amplify them with magick, you can grow in your witchcraft practice in just the same way that mineral-rich soil supports the growth of herbs. Herbs are more potent when grown in a nutrient-rich soil, and any expression of beauty will be more potent when it arises from a foundation of magick. You can take in this power, bestowed upon you by the earth, and transform it through the skills of your craft. Creating your own herbal beauty products is a magickal way to celebrate your power.

Like a wild garden, witches refuse to be defined by the conventional standards of beauty. We come in all shapes and sizes, colors, and ages. While some define beauty as the blushing maiden, others are drawn to black lipstick and winged eyeliner. If glitter and glitz is your cup of tea, your results will be even more magickal when you start from a natural herbal base. The bottom line is witches are wild and no one can define our beauty but us. It is not superimposed upon us by some outside source. It radiates from within as we glory in life.

Herbal beauty magick is simply the foundation of the personal expression of your desired aesthetic. After all, beauty is a celebration of the individual, an honoring of the spirit. Far from being superficial, witches recognize the mind, body, and spirit connection and see beauty as a natural part of it. Honoring the body is an act of magick.

Using herbs can amplify your beauty and encourage subtle yet unmistakable transformations to take place. Herbs can be used to soothe irritated skin, exfoliate, de-stress, and pamper your skin and hair. This chapter will walk you through simple preparations that will give subtle visual results and undeniable magickal results. While honoring the corporeal body, beauty spells include herbal hair rinses and their expected effects, recipes to brighten the eyes, salves and ointments for clearer skin, and dream sachets for beauty sleep and the manifestation of dreams. Take back your power and dare to define beauty for yourself, inside and out.

Some of the potent herbs that are useful to include in spells and topical preparations include:

- **Aloe:** Soothing and cooling, used to address overheated, stressed skin or skin that has been overexposed to the sun.
- **Arnica:** Accelerates healing and is often used in homeopathy.
- **Borage:** Makes an excellent facial steam for dry skin, opening pores and brightening the complexion.

- **Calendula:** One of the most widely used herbs in skincare, calendula can soothe irritated skin, minimize and heal acne, and reduce inflammations caused by common skin problems such as rosacea.
- **Chamomile:** A calming herb that has a sedative effect when taken internally. Used in hair rinses for light hair and also for skincare.
- **Comfrey:** Reduces inflammation when used as a topical. Not for internal use.
- **Honey:** Used for its topical healing properties.
- **Hypericum:** Also known as St. John's wort, hypericum is used as a mood elevator. When you begin to feel better, you look better. Hypericum has been used to counteract the effects of depression.
- **Lavender:** Often called the "woman's herb," lavender is a key ingredient in herbal beauty because it has a stimulating effect at the cellular level. Applications with lavender oil are used to address dry skin. It also has antiseptic properties and is well known for its calming effect.
- **Rosemary:** Aids memory and rejuvenates, and its aromatic needles are known to reduce headaches. Used in hair rinses for dark hair.
- **Tea tree:** Powerful antiseptic herb that accelerates healing when used in a topical.
- **Walnut:** Rich in uridine, walnuts also contribute to a sense of well-being when eaten. Uridine helps make up nucleic acids and is a proven mood elevator. The crushed hulls can also be used in exfoliants and as an ingredient in hair rinses for dark hair.

BASIC BEAUTY SPELL

Before you begin creating any of the potions and concoctions in the rest of this chapter, it is important to do so within the context of spellcraft. First, go to your altar or sacred space and set your intention. You will need:

- Stick incense
- 1 cup water
- White candle
- Powerful image (for example, a goddess with whom you resonate or an image that is aesthetically pleasing to you)
- Small white cloth
- Herbs you will be using

1. Place the incense, water, candle, and image in the directional quadrants. Leave the center area open for your magick spell.
2. Place the white cloth in the center and measure and spread your herbs upon it. White is indicative of clarity; it is the color that contains all colors of the spectrum within itself. Allow yourself to enter into a meditative state as you hold your hands over the herbs. Connect with your breath and the symbiotic relationship that you share with the plant world and give thanks for the essence, power, and life force of your herbs. Send this gratitude out through your hands and into the herbs.
3. Meanwhile, as you continue to breathe, you may envision channels of light running through your body. This is the source of your inner beauty, and you project it outwardly that it may be magnified and returned to you.
4. As you infuse your herbs with your individual energy signature, form your intention. Set your intention so that it is clear as a crystal in your mind and speak it aloud. Some examples you can use alone or combine are:

   - I come to the altar of power seeking beauty
   - I am that which I seek
   - Beauty is within me
   - Beauty surrounds me
   - What I seek I have discovered within myself
   - May it be pleasing to all
   - May it be deeply felt
   - I am the source and keeper of this beauty
   - I radiate it outward for the benefit of all beings

5. As always, end with, "So mote it be."

Now that you have spoken sacred words and begun your spellcraft, it is time for the practical application. Using your consecrated herbs, begin with the basic preparation instructions, paying attention to the ratios using your own unit of measure. It is wiser to create small batches so that they can be used and replenished rather than lingering in your refrigerator and spoiling.

MAGICKAL HERBAL HAIR CARE

Hair is one of the most magickally charged substances used in witchcraft. It can be used to summon, conjure, bind, repel, and hex. In addition:

- Hair has deep mythological, spiritual, and psychic associations—it is a symbol of beauty, virility, and strength. Sif, the wife of Thor in Norse mythology, is described as having long golden hair that flowed to her feet. And in Greek mythology, the goddess Aphrodite transforms Medusa's hair into snakes as punishment for boasting that her beauty rivaled that of the goddess. In the Bible, we are reminded of the power of hair in the story of Samson, whose strength enabled him to overcome a lion with his bare hands, a strength attributed to the fact that a razor had never touched his hair.

- Hair has protective properties—it prevents contaminants from coming into contact with the body and protects your head from the rays of the sun.

- Hair also enables you to extend your sensory perception—you can feel things through your hair before entities come into contact with your skin. Receptors that surround the hair follicles of your scalp and body increase your level of awareness by allowing you to experience your environment beyond the sensations of sight and touch.

- Hair is sensual and erotic—in Egyptian mythology, Isis is said to have spread her hair over Osiris before bringing him back to life, and Egyptian women would leave their hair unkempt as a sign of mourning.

- Hair is even considered a link to the dead, as is evidenced in the memento mori hair art that was so popular during the Victorian era. Locks of hair of the deceased were used in jewelry and picture frames, bringing comfort to those on the living side of the veil.

With all of these strong connections, it's clear to see how taking care of your hair is a magickal act. Imbuing your hair with magick is an act of self-love and self-care and can be used as a consecration rite for beauty.

The following basic herbal hair rinse will require a blend of dried herbs and some fruit infused in spring water. An herbal rinse will not change your hair color, but it will strengthen and add shine and enhance any natural highlights you have. The initial preparation will be concentrated. You can then add the desired amount to your rinse water and store the rest for up to a week. If your hair is coarse, you can also make a leave-in conditioner made from a blend of essential and carrier oils.

Basic Herbal Hair Rinses
You will need:

- 1 gallon spring water, divided
- Medium saucepan
- 1-quart glass jar
- 2 cups herbal blend (see following lists for different hair type blends)
- Strainer
- Large pitcher
- Cheesecloth
- Large scrying bowl or dark-colored glass bowl (black or cobalt)
- Tub or sink large enough to hold the bowl

To Amplify Dark Hair

- ½ cup rosemary needles
- ½ cup red raspberry leaf
- ¼ cup garden sage leaves
- ¼ cup nettle leaves
- ¼ cup calendula flowers
- ¼ cup comfrey leaf

To Amplify Fair or Light Hair

- ½ cup chamomile flowers
- ½ cup yarrow flowers and leaves
- Juice of 3 fresh lemons
- ¼ cup garden sage leaves
- ¼ cup nettle leaves
- ¼ cup calendula flowers
- ¼ cup comfrey leaves

To Amplify Auburn Hair

- 2 cups hibiscus flowers
- 1 cup red clover leaves and flowers
- ¼ cup nettle leaves
- ¼ cup calendula flowers
- ¼ cup comfrey leaves
- ¼ cup red henna powder

1. Bring 4 cups spring water to boil in the medium saucepan. Turn off the heat.

2. Prepare the glass jar by turning it under hot running water for at least 1 minute in order to warm it up. (If you are not using tempered glass, it is extremely important to bring the temperature of the glass jar up before adding your herbs so that adding hot water will not shock the glass and cause it to shatter.)

3. Fill the quart jar with the herbal blend, depending on your hair color.

4. Pour the boiled spring water over the herbs and close the jar. Allow the herbs to steep for at least 30 minutes.

5. During this time, you can ground and center yourself and attune with the magickal properties of your hair:

   - Touch your hair and notice its texture and length. Do you run your hand across it, or pull your fingers through it? Pay attention to the subtle sensations that your hair allows you to feel.

   - Your hair surrounds the area known as the crown chakra. (Hair is often referred to as "crowning glory.") Concentrate on your crown chakra. The crown chakra is considered the point of highest spiritual awakening in the auric body, located at the top of the head. You can envision the crown chakra as a purple spinning disc that opens in much the same way the pupils of your eyes dilate. Picture your crown chakra opening to allow for a spiritual awakening or communion with divine energy.

   - Allow yourself to experience your hair as an extension of your magickal being. Hair is a veil. It is a mystical substance, the part of ourselves that we shed but still associate with beauty.

   - Hair is a part of our identity. It is a record of our past and carries our DNA. How we treat our hair can be indicative of how we feel about ourselves. Think of the stories your hair contains and how it signifies your identity and in what ways.

6. After your herbal blend has steeped and the infusion is ready, notice how the color of the water in the jar has changed. Place the strainer over the pitcher and line the strainer with the cheesecloth. Pour the contents of the quart jar slowly over the strainer and cloth and into the pitcher. Gather up the herbs and squeeze any remaining liquid into the pitcher.

7. Transfer the infusion in the pitcher back into the jar.

8. Place your scrying bowl in the tub or in a deep sink.

9. Add 1½ quarts spring water to the pitcher and add 1 cup herbal infusion to the spring water in the pitcher. Your herbal rinse is now ready to use.

10. Position your head over the bowl in the tub or sink. Pour the pitcher of herbal rinse slowly over your hair so that you catch it in the bowl. Put the pitcher down and massage your scalp and pull the rinse through your hair. Squeeze out any excess from your hair into the bowl.

11. Transfer the rinse from the bowl back to the pitcher and repeat 9 times. As you rinse each time, keep the following thoughts at the top of your mind or use them as an incantation.

> "I BLESS THE PAST, MY HISTORY IS CONTAINED IN MY HAIR
> I REFLECT ON THE PAST AND ACCEPT THE LESSONS
> AND THE SCARS THAT I BEAR
> I HONOR THE LESSONS WITH WHICH I'VE BEEN BLESSED
> I ALLOW MYSELF TO GROW AND TO REST
> I NOURISH MYSELF AND BRING NUTRIENTS TO MY CROWN
> I GIVE THANKS TO THE HERBS, THE EARTH'S BEAUTIFUL GOWN
> I GIVE THANKS FOR THE FIRE THAT GLOWS AS IT WARMS
> I ACCEPT MY OWN BEAUTY IN ALL OF ITS FORMS
> I ACCEPT MY CREATIVITY AND ALLOW IT TO SHINE
> ALL THAT I AM REFLECTS THE GODDESS DIVINE."

12. When you are finished nourishing your hair with the herbal rinse, allow your hair to dry naturally in the sun and wind. Do not rinse your hair with tap water; leave the herbal infusion to do its magick. Notice and allow yourself to experience the natural energy that your hair has absorbed from the herbs. Pick out your curls or comb your hair, allowing your touch to create a feeling of self-acceptance and joy. Let the natural phenomena of your environment be a part of this beauty spell as you allow the herbal rinse to dry naturally.

13. The rest of the herbal infusion can be kept in the jar and stored in the refrigerator for future use. It will keep for a week so that you will have enough to use it every other day until it is gone. If you do not want to use the rinse throughout the week, you can use an ice cube tray to freeze it and then add the cubes to your spring water. The spring water can be kept at room temperature

and the frozen infusion added. As the ice cubes melt, they will diffuse through the water. You can also warm the spring water if you wish, but be mindful of temperature, because you do not want to inflict any scalds or burns on yourself.

Herbal Hair Rinse As a Coven Initiatory Rite

The hair rinsing ritual can also be incorporated into initiatory rites. The initiate can receive the rinse, which is done by one or two other coven members with the high priestess overseeing and proclaiming an alternative blessing as:

> "BLESS THE PAST, HISTORY IS CONTAINED IN YOUR HAIR
> REFLECT ON THE PAST AND ACCEPT THE LESSONS
> AND THE SCARS THAT YOU BEAR
> HONOR THE LESSON WITH WHICH YOU'VE BEEN BLESSED
> ALLOW YOURSELF TO GROW AND TO REST
> NOURISH THYSELF WITH NUTRIENTS TO THY CROWN
> GIVE THANKS TO THE HERBS, THE EARTH'S BEAUTIFUL GOWN
> GIVE THANKS FOR THE FIRE THAT GLOWS AS IT WARMS
> ACCEPT YOUR OWN BEAUTY IN ALL OF ITS FORMS
> ACCEPT YOUR CREATIVITY AND ALLOW IT TO SHINE
> AND ALL THAT YOU ARE REFLECTS THE GODDESS DIVINE."

This process can be a part of or in lieu of the ritual bath, which is a common preparatory rite preceding initiation.

HERBAL CROWN FOR BEAUTY, ADORNMENT, AND HONOR

Creating an herbal crown is an important task to master, as it will add dignity and authenticity to your rites and rituals. The herbal crown is a symbol of the priesthood, usually worn in coven craft by the high priestess to identify her rank. Crowns are also used during sacred rites. Participants in a handfasting ritual may wear crowns of leaves and flowers, and crowns are worn by expectant witches awaiting the birth of their child during the blessing way ritual.

The Laurel Crown

The laurel crown has its roots in the myth of Apollo, who pursued the nymph Daphne. She called upon the goddess to come to her aid, and Gaia (different versions of the myth say she called upon either Gaia or her father, a river god) turned her into a tree, creating the first dryad and an ensuing tradition of priestesses dedicated to the spirits of the trees. To show his continued devotion to Daphne, Apollo wore a crown of laurel leaves from the tree she became. The laurel crown became a hallowed symbol and was also used to celebrate Olympian athletes who brought glory through their prowess and ability.

Creating an herbal crown is an empowering act. Choose specific herbs that will energetically align with your purpose. Following, you will find instructions on how to craft an herbal crown suitable for handfasting and spring to summer sabbats. It includes herbs of attainment, purity, and sexuality in an authentic representation of the tenets of witchcraft.

To make this modern version of the classical ancient laurel crown, you will need between 10 and 20 sprigs of each of these fresh herbs, including the wick branches and stems where possible. (The exact quantity of herbs will depend on the circumference of the crown. This can be learned by taking a measure of the diameter of the person's head for which the crown is intended and factoring in the length of your herbs.) Try to have at least 1½–3 inches of stem to work with. You can also make a U-shaped crown that is open at the front; however, for symbolic reasons and ritual purposes, the unbroken circle is the preferable design. If you are making one for yourself, pay close attention to your preferred head placement. Decide beforehand if you will want to wear it straight across your forehead or tilted up to your hairline and across the base of your skull, because this may affect the diameter of the crown.

You will need:

- Green floral wire
- Wire cutters or heavy-duty scissors
- Chain nose pliers
- Green floral tape
- 10–20 sprigs bay laurel

- 10–20 sprigs sage
- 10–20 sprigs savory
- 1 or 2 large blossoms such as dahlia, peony, or daisy, among others, depending on your taste (optional)
- Hot glue gun (optional)
- Ribbon (optional)

1. Begin by bending the wire into a circle. Check the circumference by placing it on your or the wearer's head. Make sure it is not too tight, but it shouldn't fall down either. The fit at this point should be slightly loose, as you will be covering the entire circle with the floral tape, which will decrease the inside diameter a little bit. Use the wire cutters or scissors, if necessary, to cut wire to fit. Twist the ends tightly together, using the pliers to bend the ends of the wires into a loop so there are no wires sticking out. Begin wrapping the tape around the twist, then continuing on a slight angle, cover the entire circle with the floral tape. Pause and check for fit, remembering that you will be adding more tape to secure the herbs.
2. Lay the circle on your altar and begin placing the herbs around it. At this point, you can decide how dense you want the crown to be. Using more sprigs will make the crown fuller and also fit a little more snugly. Alternate the herbs so that you have a variety of color and texture next to each other. Play a little bit with the layout before you begin securing the herbs down. Make sure the herbs overlap so that as much of the wire armature as possible is covered.
3. Place the herbs so that they present on the outside facing edge of the circle. Use the floral tape to secure the sprigs to the circle. Alternate the savory and sage, interspersing the bay laurel as you go. Wrap each stem and then layer each sprig so that it covers the taped stem of the sprig in front of it.
4. If you wish, place a large blossom on the side and secure with either floral tape or a dab of hot glue. You can also add a length of ribbon for decoration, either tying it all the way around the crown or tying a bow and securing it in one place with hot glue.

Wear your crown in beauty and power, adding the magickal influence of herbs to your practice.

THE FIVE-FOLD BLESSING FOR BEAUTY

This Five-Fold blessing is a variation on the Five-Fold kiss used in traditional Alexandrian and Gardnerian Wiccan initiatory rites for witches who seek to dedicate themselves to their craft. Each component can be used as an individual spell, depending on the need of the particular practitioner. It is meant to honor tradition because it is based on a sacred rite, but it is flexible and can be used as part of a grander ritual or as a simple self-blessing for a solitary witch. This herbal variation includes eye brighteners, lip scrubs, heart warmers, perfumes, and lotions to enhance your witchy beauty.

Herbal Beauty Blessing of the Eyes

It is said that the eyes are the windows of the soul. The eyes enchant, they gaze, and they can capture a gaze as well. The eye itself does not see; the eye transmits images to the brain and it is the brain that sees. Psychic ability is often referred to as the "sight." The eye is perceptive and keen. How often do we interpret the images our eyes transmit as reality? How much of what we see is a manifestation of what we desire to see?

The magickal associations with the eyes are numerous, from the plumed peacock of the goddess Hera with one thousand eyes in its tail to the concept of the third eye, of seeing beyond. Those with the gift of prophecy are referred to as "seers" and the depictions of the eyes as portals to power are many. Think of the Utchat Eye of Horus or the ward of the Evil Eye as examples.

Blessing the eyes can be done to acknowledge your own way of seeing, or it can also be used to influence the way you are seen. This spell is meant to allow the witch to increase confidence, accept beauty, and invoke the acknowledgment and respect of others in order to be seen as a magickal being. You will need:

- 3–4 tablespoons dried eyebright
- 2 cups distilled boiled water
- ½ cup milk
- Medium bowl
- White cloth
- 2 cucumber slices
- Small amethyst crystal
- 3" × 4" muslin pouch
- ¼ cup dried lavender blossoms

1. Steep the dried eyebright in the boiled water. Combine 2 cups infusion with the milk and allow it to cool to the touch.
2. Pour the mixture into a bowl and place it upon your altar. Dip a white cloth into the warm potion to make a compress. Wring it out so that it is not dripping and fold the compress gently before laying it across your eyes. As you feel the warmth, you can whisper or speak aloud the spell:

> "THE BEAUTY THAT I FEEL WITHIN,
> MAY OTHERS SEE WITHOUT.
> MAY I ACHIEVE A PLACE OF PEACE,
> FAR FROM SHAME OR DOUBT.
> I SHOW FORTH BEAUTY IN MY WORK,
> GRACED BY MAGICK'S HAND.
> MAY THE BEAUTY OF THE WITCH ARISE
> A FLOWER FROM THE LAND.
> THE ASPECT OF BEAUTY, I INVOKE
> TO SEE AND TO BE SEEN
> LET ALL WHOSE GAZE MY EYES SHALL MEET
> REGARD ME AS A QUEEN."

Wring out the compress and repeat the process until you have gained the healing benefit of the herbs. Do not pour the remaining liquid down the sink; rather, use it to nourish your garden or the earth. Alternately, you can refrigerate it for up to seven days if you wish to repeat or share the blessing.

3. After you experience the warmth of the compress, you may want to cool down with cucumber slices over the eyes. You can relax and meditate and open your third eye by placing the amethyst in the muslin pouch and then filling the pouch with dried lavender blossoms.
4. Lie down and relax and love your eyes as you enter a meditative state. Think about your eye color and how your eyes enable and promote your perception by communicating to your mind. Are your eyes the color of the rich, brown earth? Or the green of sea, the blue of sky? Are your eyes a kaleidoscope of many colors like the beauty of the garden? If you have visual issues or impairments, be comforted by the fact that it is the mind that truly sees. Hold the pouch or balance it over your third eye and breathe in the scent of the lavender. Allow yourself to experience visions and

interpret these messages as reality. Be prepared to see yourself in a new light and allow yourself to embrace your individual beauty while cultivating the confidence to let other people see it too.

Herbal Lip Scrub

Witches know that speaking a spell, chant, wish, or dream out loud lends it power. The word is bound to the spell, and words that pass through the lips are just as effective, or even more so, than the written word because sound creates a vibrational energy that the universe receives. The lips then become a sacred part of the spell, and treating the lips magickally will enhance their appearance and their power.

With this magickal lip scrub, words of power spoken aloud have never been sweeter. The combination of honey, sugar, and coconut oil creates a hydrating and exfoliating effect, giving you the lips of a goddess. You will need:

- 2 teaspoons of granulated organic sugar
- ½ teaspoon wildflower honey
- ⅛ teaspoon vitamin E oil
- 1 or 2 drops diluted herbal oil of your choice (for example, mint leaves infused in jojoba oil or a dilution of essential oil into a carrier)
- ⅛ teaspoon coconut oil
- 2 drops vanilla extract
- Small metal 1-ounce jar

1. Combine the sugar and honey in a small glass bowl. Add in the vitamin E oil and the herb-infused oil and coconut oil. Mix well.
2. Add in 2 drops vanilla and combine well to make a thick paste.
3. Take a small amount on your fingertips and roll it across your lips. The paste will bead up and distribute evenly across your lips while the granulated sugar helps slough off dried or dead skin. Continue to roll the paste around your lips in a circle. Repeat the motion as you meditate on these words:

"LIPS THAT PART
LIPS THAT SPEAK
THE WORDS OF THE HEART
THE BEAUTY I SEEK
WORDS OF POWER

WORDS OF PRAISE
BLESSINGS OF FLOWERS
ENERGY I RAISE
MY WORD WILL BE TRUE
THE MAGICK WILL COME
IN ALL THAT I DO
SO MUST IT BE DONE."

4. As you meditate on the charm, allow your lips to absorb the healing oils and the sweetness of the honey and sugar. When you have completed the charm, lick off any excess and enjoy the feeling of your soft and plump lips.

5. Transfer the rest of the paste to the 1-ounce container. Since the honey and sugar impede the growth of bacteria through virtue of their sweetness, your potion does not need to be refrigerated. It can be used as often as you like.

Herbal Beauty Blessing of the Heart

The heart chakra resonates with the color green, making an herbal blessing a perfect attunement for blessing the heart. This herbal charm can be worn around the neck to bring about balance and harmony. You will need:

- 4" × 6" drawstring muslin pouch
- ¼ cup flax seeds
- Small jar with lid
- 2 drops jasmine essential oil
- 3 tablespoons dried lavender blossoms
- Dried roses; either 9 miniature dried rosebuds or 1 tablespoon dried petals
- 1 yard red silk cord, around 3 millimeters in diameter

1. Fill the muslin pouch halfway full with flax seeds. Transfer the seeds to the jar and add jasmine. Close the jar and shake vigorously to allow the oil to disperse through the seeds. Transfer the oiled seeds back to the pouch.

2. Fill the rest of the pouch with the lavender and roses. Shake gently to mix the dried flowers and seeds.

3. Tie the pouch securely in a double bow knot and run the red cord through the loops. Tie the ends of the cord together so that the charm can be worn around your neck, resting at around 20 inches, or heart level. You can even heat it up for 15 seconds in a microwave for a truly heartwarming charm.

Herbal Beauty Blessing of the Sex

Herbs are actually quite sexual—some of them are very cunning in their techniques of seduction, luring pollinators with their scent and appearance. Think of the myriad shapes and forms of flowers and of how beautifully they resemble human sex organs. Pistils and stamens, blossoms and seed pods are all testament to the divine connection between humankind and nature, between the beauty of sexual expression and the sacredness of the sensual.

A large part of magickal workings are the symbolic and sympathetic relationships between entities. In the Wiccan oracle widely known as The Charge of the Goddess, the oracle explicitly states that all acts of love and pleasure are representative of the witch's path and are considered sacred acts of devotion. Blessing your sex, no matter how it manifests inwardly or outwardly, is an act of self-love well in keeping with the tenets of witchcraft. Invoking sexuality is as normal as the duality in nature. It represents the life-giving force that enlivens the earth.

To prepare a blessing of the sex, create an anointing oil that will nourish your skin and will feel and smell pleasant. Some suggested essential oil blends for this recipe are:

Feminine Oil Blend

- Base note (the scent that will last the longest and is the foundation of the blend): 15 drops oak moss
- Middle note (harmonizes with and blends together the base and top notes): 10 drops gardenia
- Top note (the fragrance that you will notice first; it will also fade the fastest): 3 drops lilac

Masculine Oil Blend
- Base note: 10 drops patchouli
- Middle note: 10 drops sandalwood
- Top note: 3 drops lavender

For the rest of the recipe, you will need:

- 1 ounce grated beeswax
- Double boiler
- 1 ounce jojoba oil
- 2 metal 1-ounce containers
- Selection of herbal essential oils. Since scent is highly individual, please experiment with scents that invoke your own pleasure. Do not think of attracting at this time. Think of what you personally enjoy, and what makes you feel comfortable and sexual.
- Flat toothpicks

1. Heat the grated beeswax in the double boiler until it is liquid. Add the jojoba oil and gently mix the two ingredients together to achieve a homogenous blend. Pour half the liquid into each container and add 3 drops of your essential oil blend. Quickly stir the mixture with the toothpicks before the wax begins to set.
2. Keep one container for anointing yourself and the other as a gift to your consort so that he or she may come to appreciate you on a new level. If you are solitary and without a consort, you can use one for anointing your skin and the other for charging candles and ritual tools.

Herbal Beauty Blessing of the Feet

Our feet come into contact with the ground more than any other part of ourselves. This herbal foot bath will help you attune more closely to the energies of the earth. It also gives you the opportunity to absorb minerals through your feet, giving you another level of attunement with the plant world. This invigorating foot bath is infused with magick as well as magnesium, which is a crucial mineral for growth of both herbs and people. You will need:

- 1 cup herbs such as mint (or peppermint, basil, thyme, or catnip)
- 1 quart boiled water
- Large container or bowl to accommodate both feet
- ¼ cup natural sea salt
- 1 cup Epsom salts
- 3 drops tea tree essential oil

1. Prepare the infusion by letting the fresh mint steep in boiled water for 30 minutes.
2. While the infusion is still very warm, transfer it to the large container or bowl. Pour in the sea salt and the Epsom salts and allow them to dissolve. Add 3 drops of tea tree essential oil.
3. Find a comfortable place to sit and allow your feel to soak. As you do, envision the following:

   - Focus all of your intention on your feet. You feel the sensation of warmth and water surrounding you. Spread out your toes, allowing the water to inhabit the spaces in between. Think of the roots of an herb; threadlike, thin, and delicate, yet capable of moving through the earth slowly and deliberately, undetected. Powerful enough to crack concrete. Sensitive enough to detect movement. Smart enough to locate nutrients and moisture. Open and wise enough to absorb only what is necessary for growth.
   - Think of what it means to put down roots and how far the path of your life has taken you up to this point. Think of the current season and its attributes. Discover how you fit into the world around you and how every square inch of soil is teeming with life. When you establish this root connection with yourself and your environment, come back to a centered state of consciousness and give your feet a blessing:

   > "BLESSED ARE MY FEET
   > THAT HAVE BROUGHT ME TO THESE WAYS
   > BLESSED BE THE NIGHTS
   > BLESSED BE THE DAYS
   > BLESSED BE THE STEPS I TAKE
   > ALONG THIS SACRED PATH
   > BLESSED BE MY FEET
   > AND BLESSED BE THE BATH."

4. When your meditation is complete and the bath is cool, you may pour it back into the earth to nourish the land.

HENNA AND ADORNING THE SKIN

The dried and ground-up leaves and seeds of the henna tree, *Lawsonia inermis*, are widely used for dyeing the hair, skin, and nails. Known as mehndi, the application of henna paste to the palms of the hands and the bottoms of the feet is part of the wedding tradition for brides, particularly those who follow the Hindu and Muslim faith.

It is important to recognize the Asian and North African origins of this tradition. Witchcraft is by nature eclectic, drawing from practices and pantheons as diverse as Celtic, Greco-Roman, Native American, African, and Germanic, to name but a few. While eclectic incorporation of goddess traditions from pre-Christian and non-Christian faiths into witchcraft is common, it is extremely important to recognize and acknowledge the origin of these traditions. Otherwise, cultural appropriation is the undesirable result. In cultural appropriation, sacred elements from the original tradition are adopted by nonpractitioners and/or nonbelievers and stripped of their sacred meaning without regard to their true purpose or their source. In witchcraft, we can incorporate eclecticism and avoid appropriation by honoring the traditions and the deities of the native land. This can be done by including naming the land and the appropriate sovereign deities during the creation of the potion.

Henna is a beautiful and popular form of body art, but its origin is sacred. In preparation for marriage, the bride's hands and feet will be painted in order to invoke prosperity and health and to summon the blessing and aid of spirits as the bride transitions from maiden to wife. It is also considered a blessing to imbed the initials of the betrothed couple into the design. Popular motifs include quatrefoils, feather patterns, peacock patterns, and floral and paisley patterns, to name but a few.

While acknowledging the origin of this sacred marriage rite, mehndi can be adapted to dye the skin as a way to imbue the witch with power. Sacred symbols can be painted onto the palms, creating a temporary tattoo that can last up to 3 weeks. Additionally, extract of henna has been proven to have antiseptic properties, making this herbal preparation a healing concoction as well. In order to create a mehndi paste for adorning and dyeing the skin, you will need:

- 4 slices tamarind fruit or 3–4 tablespoons tamarind paste
- ¾ cup fresh or dried red rose petals
- ⅛ cup coffee grounds
- 1 dried lime (prepare this 2–3 weeks in advance; the lime can be sliced to expedite drying)
- Medium saucepan
- 1 quart spring water

- Small glass jar
- Strainer lined with cheesecloth
- Parchment paper and pen
- Scissors
- Nylon stocking for use as a sieve
- 4 ounces dried and powdered red henna
- Small mixing bowl
- 3 drops eucalyptus essential oil
- 2 fresh okra pods
- Small wooden spoon
- Jacquard craft bottles with 2-millimeter tip
- Straight pin
- Cotton and plastic wrap

1. Place the tamarind, rose petals, coffee grounds, and dried lime in the saucepan. Cover with spring water. Bring up heat slowly. Create a decoction by allowing the mixture to simmer on low heat for at least half an hour, taking care to keep the decoction covered so that the liquid doesn't evaporate. Turn off the heat and let the decoction cool to room temperature.
2. Prepare a jar to catch the decoction. Strain the decoction by pouring it through the strainer lined with cheesecloth. Gather the drained remnants in the cheesecloth and squeeze into the jar to catch any remaining liquid. Set the decoction aside.
3. Take the parchment paper and pen and write down your sigils and spells on the paper. You can be clear and specific about your intent and the symbols you wish to use. Elementals, zodiacal, planetary, and symbols and sigils of your own creation are appropriate. As you write, you can add your specifics into this basic spell framework:

> "PASSED DOWN FROM WOMAN TO WOMAN
> OUR CONNECTION IS ONE OF SKIN TO SKIN
> FROM MANY LANDS, FROM MANY DREAMS
> AND MANY HANDS WASHED IN MANY STREAMS
> THE SPELL MUST NOW BEGIN
> FROM HEART TO HAND AND HERB TO LAND
> I BLESS THE SKIN IN WHICH I LOVE
> AS IT IS BELOW, SO MUST IT BE ABOVE."

The Modern Witchcraft Guide to Magickal Herbs

4. Place the inscribed parchment paper on the floor under two legs of a chair. Sit in front of the chair and using a scissors, cut along the length of the nylon stocking. Tie one end to the chair leg closest to you and tie the other end to the chair leg behind the one in front of you, making a taut little hammock through which to sift the henna powder. Pour the henna powder into the stocking and run your hands back and forth through it, pressing it through the stocking and allowing it to fall onto the parchment. Repeat until all the stems and large pieces of cellulose have been removed.

5. Carefully gather up the sides of the parchment and slide then tap the sifted henna powder into a clean and dry bowl. Gradually add the decoction 1 tablespoon at a time until the mixture resembles a thick lotion. It should be moist but not runny at all.

6. Add 3 drops eucalyptus oil and mix it in. Slice the okra and force it through the cheesecloth, adding the slimy liquid of the pods to the henna paste. Use the wooden spoon to mix it all together thoroughly and transfer it to the bottles. An easy way to do this is to squeeze the air out of the bottle, then hold the mouth of the squeezed bottle into the henna paste and release your grip on it, allowing it to expand and suck up some of the paste. Tap the bottom of the bottle on the floor so that the paste settles on the bottom and then very gently squeeze the air out again and repeat until the bottle is relatively full.

7. Wipe off any excess and then screw the tip onto the bottle and begin tracing over your symbols and sigils on the parchment to practice before applying the paste to your skin. The skin of the palms and the bottoms of the feet absorb the dye most readily, and it will appear darker on these areas than it will on other parts of the body.

8. Keep a straight pin close by in case the tip gets clogged. Loosen any stray material by clearing the tip with the pin. You can now begin applying the henna paste to your skin. Allow it to dry thoroughly and keep the design safe by covering it carefully with cotton and then wrapping your skin with a plastic wrap to keep the cotton in place. The longer you allow the henna paste to dye your skin, the darker your design will be. You may opt to leave it on overnight.

9. When the paste is thoroughly dry, brush it off gently. Do not wash it off with water. The design will darken as it oxidizes and will last for approximately 3 weeks.

Chapter 6

APHRODISIACS AND ATTRACTION: HERBAL CHARMS FOR LOVE

L ove and the desire for love are often what brings practitioners into witchcraft. This chapter will teach you about the sensual side of herbs and how attracting love, deepening love, awakening love, and self-love can be enhanced with herbal knowledge. Herbs have been used to amplify the feelings of love for centuries across many continents such as Asia and Europe.

The Greek goddess of love, known as Venus or Aphrodite, is credited with gifting humankind with aphrodisiacs. Derived from one of the sacred names of the goddess, aphrodisiacs should be considered part of a magickal expression. In the Charge of the Goddess, the oracle affirms that "all acts of love and pleasure are mine." Herbal aphrodisiacs are a potent form of magick, as they connect witches with the erotic energy of the earth. The earth is supple and moist in the springtime. It brings forth all manner of life and fruit. At Beltane, the scent of hawthorn blossoms ignites desire as the lord and lady unite in their sacred, life-giving embrace. From experiencing acts of pleasure to setting the stage for desire, herbal magick can be used to bring a sensual element to your witchcraft.

AWAKENING APHRODITE THROUGH SCENT

Calling upon the goddess of love is an integral part of witchcraft. It is important to note immediately that any type of manipulative magick is ill advised. If the one you seek is not seeking you, then any spell you create is likely to result in a passing fancy and not a true bond of love. Even with that caveat, it is still possible and even preferable to take control of one's environment and create an aura of attraction.

One way to encourage love is through scent. The olfactory system is designed to pick up on pleasurable unseen entities, and herbs play an integral role in this. Scent is a powerful aspect of attraction and has a rich psychology attached to it. Many believe that scent is more attractive than physical appearance. Some scents that are associated with attraction include sandalwood, jasmine, and patchouli. You can create an environment of romance and seduction, which can heighten desire by the strategic use of herbs. Set the stage for love with a selection of herbs that will be pleasing and fragrant.

Scenting a room can be done a number of ways: with incense, aromatherapy, and potpourri. Exploring the sensual nature of scent with herbal spells and blessings will add magick to your love life. Capturing a fragrance is not difficult and the scent does not have to be short-lived. Creating your own potpourri blend is a sensual way to start.

A potpourri blend contains three parts:

- **A signature scent:** You will choose this based on what resonates strongly with you, the scent that draws you out of yourself and leads you to thoughts of pleasure.
- **A blender:** A blender is an additional scent that complements the signature scent. You may wish to experiment until you find a sensual balance. A nice blender to add to a signature scent would be something resinous to balance out a floral scent. For example, you may be drawn to rose or to lavender as a signature scent but then add clove as a blender to spice things up.
- **A fixative:** A fixative is an herb that is powdered or cut, then used to coat the signature scent and the blender. It helps the scent last for years.

Potpourri can be kept in an open bowl or in a lidded jar and opened only on special occasions. This particular blend is perfect for the bedroom. You will need:

- Large bowl
- 1 cup dried lavender flowers
- 1 cup dried rose petals and rosebuds
- 1 cup dried jasmine flowers
- 1 vanilla bean
- 2–3 drops lavender essential oil

- Pinch orris root powder
- Glass bowl
- Glass jar with lid

1. In a large bowl, gently mix all of the dried flowers together to blend. Cut or chop up the vanilla bean and add it to the mix. Add 2 or 3 drops lavender oil and sprinkle the mixture with a pinch of orris root powder.
2. Place the potpourri in an attractive glass dish or shallow bowl by your bedside and keep the remainder fresh in a glass jar with a tight-fitting lid.

Orris Root Powder: The Root of Beauty

Orris root refers to the roots of several species of iris flowers such as *Iris germanica* and *Iris pallida*. These types of flowers were named for a Greek goddess. Known as "Iris of the Rainbow," Iris was represented as a flower maiden and was known as a messenger of the gods. Orris root has a scent similar to violet and is often used in cosmetics and perfumes because of its ability to stabilize and enhance other fragrances. Using orris root in your magick means that you are seeking a stable relationship rooted in beauty and communication.

LOVE OF THE SELF

Expressions of self-love are acts of courage, including the courage of owning and loving your body. We are constantly being bombarded with unattainable images of romantic love. It is rarely easy, takes constant work, and is seldom anything but the heteronormative monogamy that is constantly being raised as the cultural ideal. Love takes many forms. The ancient Greek philosophers had several words for love. Among the best known is *agape*, which refers to the unconditional love between gods, goddesses, and mortals. Even Christians use *agape* to describe the love of God for his followers. There are other types of love. Filial love is the love between parent and child, which comes from the Greek *philae*, affectionate love. Eros, also known as Cupid, is the source of erotic love. And philautia is the often overlooked concept of self-love. Philautia call us to be compassionate and accepting of ourselves in a healthy way that is neither narcissistic or self-centered to the exclusion of others.

Love involves being or allowing ourselves to become vulnerable. To love demands a willingness to accept first ourselves and then others. It is imperative that this equation is honored, for in the Charge of the Goddess, the oracle states, "If that which you seek you find not within yourself, you will never find it without." Thus, the first step before manifesting external love, be it through a relationship, creative endeavor, or showing forth works in the world, is the manifestation of self-love. To love yourself is to trust yourself. It means you must be accepting of your own curiosity and open to experiencing sensations. The power of desire is strong and must be regarded with care. When you take desire and regard it as a sacred expression, it takes on deeper significance and new meaning on the path of magickal self-discovery and how we express our sensuality.

Herbs for Radiating Love Outwardly

If you want to project an aura of love, add a matrix of fresh flowers and herbs to your altar. An herbal matrix is similar to a flower mandala, but it is created with the intention to align the energy signature of herbs with the desire to invoke. The matrix will have a central focal point with rays that extend outward. The rays are the points at which love is radiated outward to be received and matched by the universe. The negative spaces in between the rays are the channels through which the energy signature is returned to its source, back to you, the creator of the matrix. You will need to clear space on your altar, at the same time symbolically clearing space in your own life to make room for love to enter in. You will need:

- Red hibiscus blossom
- 8 pieces dried cinnamon bark
- 8 sprigs rosemary
- Yarrow
- Rosebuds or rose petals

1. At the center of the matrix, place the red hibiscus blossom. The first set of rays will be sticks of dried cinnamon bark in an equidistant pattern of eight surrounding the hibiscus blossom. In between each cinnamon ray, you will position a slender rosemary sprig, increasing the surface area of the matrix.

2. Around the outer perimeter defined by the rosemary, you will position clusters of yarrow. Be sure that the clusters do not touch each other. You want to create space for love to enter in.

3. In the negative spaces in between the rays of cinnamon and rosemary, you can add the rosebuds or rose petals, taking care not to create any blockages.

4. Meditate with your matrix, accepting the beauty you have shown forth in the world and acknowledging the space you have made for love.

INVOKING ERATO WITH AN ANOINTING POTION

Of the Camenae, the sacred muses who governed the arts, the most sexual is Erato, the muse of erotic poetry. That erotic poetry would have a dedicated muse is indicative of the importance of sensuality and its intersection with divinity during the classical era. Unlike Abrahamic religions in which expressions of sexuality are taboo, in witchcraft, sexuality is celebrated as a life-giving and sacred part of human existence. To invoke Erato is to welcome sexual love into your life. You can use herbs to amplify this power by making an erotic anointing potion. You will need:

- Cheesecloth for straining
- ¼ cup damiana
- ¼ cup ginkgo
- Kola nut
- Lovage root
- 2 clean (16-ounce) glass jars with a tight-fitting lids
- 1 to 1½ cups sweet almond oil, enough to cover all herbs

1. Place all the herbs into one of the jars and completely cover them with the almond oil. Label the jar with the date and allow the herbs to infuse for 6 weeks. At the end of 6 weeks, use the cheesecloth to strain the infused oil into the second jar. When you are ready to use your enchanting oil, you can anoint a candle as well as your pulse points such as your neck and the insides of your wrists. Use the following invocation to bring power to your spell or charm:

> "WITHIN ME, YOU HAVE IGNITED A FLAME
> WITH THIS SPARK OF PASSION

I CALL UPON THE SACRED NAME
ERATO! I INVOKE AND INVITE YOU
FILL MY BODY WITH CELESTIAL FIRE
WITH LOVE AND REVERENCE
YOUR POWER TO INSPIRE
AND ALLOW ME THE MEANS
TO FULFILL MY DESIRE."

HERBS TO BOOST LIBIDO AND LUST

There are many herbs credited with enhancing sexual desire. Before any herbal work takes place, however, it is important to understand exactly what you are intending to invoke. There are numerous anecdotes of witches who attempt magick to influence a partner's desire and then end up with more than they bargained for! There are also common stories of witches who invoke a lover, but the invocations are not specific enough and the practitioner may end up with an abundance of interested partners who are of little interest to the spellcaster. As with any magickal working, especially those incorporating herbs since herbs are living beings, setting your intention in as specific terms as possible is the first step to achieving a magickal success.

Once you know exactly what you want, you can begin thinking about which herbs best fit your goal. Here are herbs associated with libido and lust and instructions on how to use them:

- **Agave:** The fermented juice intoxicates and stimulates erotic desire. The syrup can be diluted in water or added to a potion such as those described in Chapter 3, including Mystic Moon Milk.
- **Basil:** Inspires confidence and a willingness to experiment sexually. The fresh leaves and flowers can be eaten or liberally included in recipes such as the Summer Sorceress Salad in Chapter 3.
- **Calamus root:** Used as an herbal bath, calamus root is used to increase virility and sexual desire.
- **Capsicum:** When a dash is added to ripe pineapple and eaten, this combination has an aphrodisiac effect.
- **Celery:** When eaten cooked or raw, it strengthens the desire for sex and prepares the body for sexual activity.
- **Cinnamon:** The diluted essential oil is used for sexual stimulation and can be applied behind the ears, on the neck, and on the lips.

- **Garlic:** When pressed and combined with coriander, the resulting mixture is used to reverse impotence caused by hexing. The mixture of pressed garlic and coriander seeds can be ritually eaten while in a meditative state to increase its effectiveness as a counter craft charm.
- **Ginger:** Ginger's accompanying heat fans the flames of passion. The fresh grated root can be infused in a tea and drunk.
- **Ginkgo:** Eating the toasted seeds can be interpreted as being open to sexual encounters. Improves sexual function in men.
- **Ginseng:** When drunk as a tonic, ginseng increases the desire for sex.
- **Horseradish:** Consumed to renew vigor after sexual intercourse.
- **Lovage:** Tonic made from the root is said to inspire lust in taciturn women.
- **Mustard seeds and greens:** Eaten to encourage virility.
- **Nutmeg:** The essential oil inspires desire. The oil can be diluted and added to a spray to consecrate a sacred sexual space or a few drops can be added to a sachet and placed under a pillow.
- **Yarrow:** Consumed as an infusion, yarrow was used as an aphrodisiac by Native Americans, either imbibed or chewed in the hours preceding intercourse.
- **Ylang-ylang:** The essential oil diluted with coconut as a carrier oil makes a seductive massage oil.
- **Yohimbe:** Dilates blood vessels contributing to male orgasm. It's sometimes brewed into a tea, but talk to your doctor before trying it.

HOMEMADE EROTIC AROMATHERAPY SPRAY

The olfactory system is incredibly complex. It is connected to both memory and desire. Aromatic herbs allow us to access and awaken the sensual world. Scent can transport us to another realm. Scent can ignite desire. Using herbs for their scent is a powerful way to enhance sexual experiences.

Remember never to use essential oils as topicals. They can be diffused in steam or a few drops can be added to an aromatherapy spray. To make an erotic aromatherapy spray, you will need:

- 2–3 drops essential oil such as:
  - Jasmine
  - Ylang-ylang
  - Rose
  - Sandalwood
  - Orange blossom
  - Clary sage
  - Fennel

- ½ cup distilled water
- 3 tablespoons witch hazel (to act as a preservative)
- Opaque glass spray bottle

1. First, familiarize yourself with the different fragrances of the essential oils and see which ones resonate with you. Scent can be very sexually stimulating, but each person is different. You don't have to use every recommendation on this list; the suggested herbs can serve as a starting point for you to discover which fragrances are effective for you.
2. Next, combine the distilled water and witch hazel in a cobalt or other opaque glass spray bottle.
3. Add a few drops of your chosen essential oils into the spray bottle. Shake gently to allow the oils to disperse in the solution, then spray the area in front of you and walk through the mist before it settles throughout the room. As you pass through the mist, you can whisper to yourself:

> "I WALK IN PASSION AND DESIRE
> I AM WORTHY OF PLEASURE
> MAY IT BE HERE NOW!"

INFUSION TO DRINK WITH YOUR PARTNER

The ritual expressions of love have long been a part of witchcraft. The Great Rite of Beltane is largely understood to be a purely sexual representation of the Goddess and her Sacred Consort joining together to ensure the fertility of the earth. From the earth, all manner of plants and animals burst forth, sustained and propagated through the Great Rite. While the need for privacy during intimacy is sacrosanct, creating love potions and rituals to enhance the experience is well within the practice of modern witchcraft. This love potion is designed to create a nourishing feeling of intimacy while employing herbs long associated with increasing desire.

You will need:

- 1 quart spring water
- 9 rose petals
- 9 orange blossoms or ⅛ teaspoon orange zest
- 2–3 drops clary sage oil

- 2 tablespoons honey or agave
- 1 cup sliced almonds
- 2–3 drops vanilla
- Blender

1. Create an infusion by boiling the spring water and adding the rose petals, orange blossoms or zest, and sage oil. Add the agave or honey while the water is still warm so that it dissolves.
2. Soak the sliced almonds in the infusion overnight. Add a few drops of vanilla and transfer to a blender to homogenize. Drink warm or cool, however you and your partner prefer.

RELAX WITH AN INTIMATE HERBAL STEAM

Using steam can bring literal heat to any relationship. Creating an herbal steam can be a relaxing and intimate shared experience. You will need:

- 1 quart water
- ⅓ cup each of lavender, rosemary, and peppermint leaves
- Towel

1. Boil the water in a medium pot and add in the herbs.
2. Lean over the infusion with your eyes closed. Have your partner drape a towel to create a tent to trap the steam so that you can inhale and feel the heat enliven your cheeks, lips, and entire face. Then, take turns and hold the towel for your partner. Admire each other's flushed appearance and appreciate the shared experience.

Chapter 7

FATE AND FORTUNE: HERBAL SPELLS AND CHARMS FOR LUCK

Money trees and spells for abundance can be enhanced with herbs. Many herbs from the mint family are considered advantageous for drawing prosperity. Even the word "mint" is used directly as a euphemism for money. To "make a mint" is to acquire great wealth. Something that "costs a mint" is considered very expensive. Even the color mint green is associated with money, and many currencies feature some shade of green. Plus, green is the color of growth, and most people want to grow their wealth. Learn about auspicious herbs for drawing money, luck, and prosperity in this chapter.

CREATING AN HERBAL MONEY TREE

The old adage that money doesn't grow on trees is certainly true, but a meditative herbal altar craft is a sincere way to focus your intention on the prosperity and abundance that you wish to invoke. By creating an herbal money tree, you create a symbol upon which to focus. The power of the herbal money tree is in its creation and then its existence. You have to prepare your mind to accept prosperity by first making room for it, then by taking action, and finally by accepting that the prosperity you seek is already yours. Too often, we focus our thoughts and energy on scarcity. Counterintuitively, that which we focus upon has the most potential for growth, even if it is something we do not truly want! Creating a money tree allows a witch to align herself with the power of herbs and, through a creative endeavor, create space for abundance to manifest. It is a simple yet powerful spell. You will need:

- Small branch or twig that resembles a tree
- Money-drawing oil (see sidebar)
- Selection of fresh herbs including basil, mint, catnip, parsley, and bay laurel
- Wire cutters
- Florist wire
- Small cauldron or pot
- Putty or a small bit of florist foam to fit in the cauldron or pot
- Selection of tumbled crystals, agates, and other semiprecious stones

1. Go for a walk in the woods in search of your branch or twig. It should resemble a tree as much as possible. It should come to you easily; you should not have to use force to break it off of a living tree. Look for a gift from nature as you become aware of your surroundings and of how perfectly nature provides for all who live in harmony and balance with her. When you have found your twig, take it home and anoint it with money-drawing oil (see sidebar).
2. Gather your herbs together and gently separate the leaves, leaving as much stem as possible.
3. Cut several lengths of wire into 1½-inch-long pieces. Wrap one end of each wire around tiny bundles of not more than three leaves. You can mix the leaves; they do not have to be bundled according to type. Wrap the bundles around the parts of the twig that look like branches, leaving one bare to serve as the trunk. As you wrap each bundle of leaves, envision precisely what it is that you want and in the specific form in which you need your prosperity to manifest. As you continue to wrap, speak your intentions out loud and do not be afraid in your petition. You are aligning your need with your desire and welding it to your action and sealing it with your word.
4. When your tree is lush, green, and abundantly covered, "plant" it in your cauldron to symbolize the cauldron of transformation. You can also use a flower pot, which is symbolic of growth. That

which you have given action and voice to on the psychic plane is implored to manifest on the physical plane. Secure it upright by placing some putty in the base of the container or using a bit of florist foam. Surround your tree with beautiful gems to anchor it.

5. Place it on your altar, your desk, your kitchen counter, or whatever auspicious location that will lend itself to the manifestation of your abundance. So mote it be!

Recipe for Money-Drawing Oil

You can create your own money-drawing oil by combining fresh basil, catnip, bay laurel, and mint in a jar and covering the fresh herbs with olive oil. This is best started during the new moon cycle. Add in a dozen clove buds and seal the jar. Let the herbs infuse for about 6 weeks. As the moon waxes full 1½ months later, strain the oil to remove the herbs and use the infusion for your spells.

THE LUCKY HAND RITUAL

Described in the works of Nigel Pennick are the spells recorded in personal grimoires from practitioners who follow in earnest the surviving traditions of Anglo Saxon witchcraft. Elements of traditional magick are still practiced today, as is evident in the many spells and charms designed to invoke luck or ward off bad luck. One such spell is the "Lucky Hand," which is an interesting bit of herbal magick. This is a relevant example of sympathetic magick in that it involves using a living plant, magickally altering it into a charm, and then bringing it into the home as a consecrated protective symbol. The symbol of the hand or hamsa as a ward against evil and fear dates back to Phoenician civilization, approximately 1000 B.C.E. and was long considered to be an emblem of the goddess. The Lucky Hand is a powerful bit of modern herbal magick that is linked symbolically to ancient pagan talismans.

Attributed to Pennick, the Lucky Hand ritual begins with the harvesting of a fern, which must be taken with the roots intact and pulled from the earth on Midsummer Eve, the pagan sabbat of Litha. Using a bolline (the white-handled knife used for practical magickal workings, not to be confused with the athalme, the double-edged blade reserved for ritual work), the magick practitioner then cuts away selected fronds of the fern, leaving behind only five in order to invoke the image of a green hand. (The pattern of five is readily observable in a multitude of plant life. Leaf and petal patterns will often occur in repetitions of five, including most varieties in the rose family, whose petals are almost always arrayed in multiples of five.) The fronds are then wafted over the smoke of a ritual fire to imbue them with elemental energy, to purify the hand as a magickal ward, and also to dry it out and strengthen it. The Lucky Hand is then taken inside the house where it is kept as a ward against bad luck.

THE BASIC WITCH'S GARDEN

A witch's garden is grown with intention. The intention can be the cultivation of herbs for spellcasting and charms, for healing, or for kitchen witchery. Typically, a witch's garden is planted in a circle, representing the circle of life: the Wheel of the Year, the earth, the sun, the moon, etc. The outer border is planted with red flowers such as hibiscus, geranium, or red nasturtiums in three or four rows and is meant to serve as a protective barrier. It is the herbal equivalent of casting a circle, the potent boundary that separates the mundane from the magickal. It might also have a water feature such as a pool, birdbath, or fountain.

Inside the circle are herbs chosen by the witch specific to the nature of her work. Some other correspondences you may want to consider are the astrological associations with certain herbs and plants. There are many ornamental flowers and sacred trees that have zodiacal associations. Some of these are:

- **Capricorn:** Nightshade, cypress, rose, and pine
- **Aquarius:** Snowdrop and foxglove
- **Pisces:** Heliotrope, willow, and elm
- **Aries:** Wild rose, chestnut, thistle, and holly
- **Taurus:** Lily of the valley, myrtle, almond, and violet
- **Gemini:** Snapdragon, filbert, and elder
- **Cancer:** Water lily, willow, and poppy
- **Leo:** Sunflower, marigold, laurel, and palm
- **Virgo:** Cornflower, valerian, and hazel
- **Libra:** White rose, violet, and almond
- **Scorpio:** Chrysanthemum, heather, and holly
- **Sagittarius:** Carnation, mulberry, and ivy vines

These correspondences are centuries old and are included to inspire your garden choices. Including a plant, tree, or herb that resonates with your zodiac sign is another way to strengthen your connection to the earth. There are other ways to create a magickal witch's garden as well. Read on for inspiration on how to plan inspired and thriving herb gardens rich with magick.

CREATE A PENTACLE HERB GARDEN

Continuing with the magickal implications of the number five, a pentacle garden can be made either upon the land or in a flower pot. This versatile herbal garden can also serve as a living altar. There are many ways to create the pentacle symbol; for example:

- You can create a pentacle with stones or gravel and fill in the negative space with herbs of your choice depending on your intention and needs.
- You can use wheatgrass to create a living pentacle. This can be accomplished by digging a shallow trough in the shape of the pentagram, either in the ground or in a container. If you are doing a ground planting, use stakes. If you are gardening in a container, use chopsticks. Place five stakes or chopsticks equidistant from each other along the circumference of a circle. Make five lines connecting each point and plant the grass seeds with the dug-out lines. Cover them lightly and mist them daily. They will sprout in a pentacle pattern, giving you a living green magickal garden.

If you are using a pot, the pot can be rotated so that the pentacle is in either the invoking and receiving position or the deflecting and protective position, depending on your needs.

PLANT A SEAL OF SOLOMON HERB GARDEN TO STRENGTHEN YOUR INTENTIONS

The Seal of Solomon has great significance in the Abrahamic religions. Its pattern of interlocking triangles holds great significance for witches too. The tenet "As above, so below" can be interpreted many ways: as a relationship between witches and the goddesses to whom they are devoted and as an agreement between the spirit world and the living. It can also be interpreted as a balance of the energies of sky and earth. Although it holds powerful spiritual significance, it also has secular interpretations about the agency of the individual: That which we invoke is parallel to that which we receive. Another important aspect of the Seal of Solomon is that by nature of its design, it also represents the elemental symbols of earth, air, water, and fire, as its pattern of triangles with transversal lines delineates.

To create the Seal of Solomon herb garden, you will need a round area or container. Begin in a similar fashion to the pentagram design, but you will mark six equidistant points instead of five. Decide how you will indicate the sigil, either with a line of stones or gravel or with planted wheatgrass. Connect the six points so that they create the interlocking triangle pattern. Then, either dig the trough lines and plant the seeds or indicate the lines with stones. Fill in the negative space with the herbs of your choice. For this project, some suggestions are endive, horehound, coriander, horseradish, parsley, and tansy. These herbs have cultural significance to the seal.

DESIGN YOUR OWN SIGIL FOR EMPOWERMENT

While the pentagram and the Seal of Solomon are two of the most powerful and best-known sigils, you can also be creative and create your own. Linear sigils are the easiest to construct, but this should not limit you in designing a personal magick herb garden for prosperity and luck. It is popular for modern witches to create their own sigils during spellwork, and if your magickal undertaking is of great significance or impact in your life (and most likely it is, otherwise you would not be invoking the aid of magick), then creating your own seal and designing an herb garden with it is a very empowering endeavor.

Use the same 6' × 6' grid described in Chapter 2 (The Personal Herbal Labyrinth) and place a letter inside each square as well as numbers zero through nine. Then, write your desire or the highest possible outcome of the situation you are currently facing, preferably in a single word. You can use the numbers if you need to apply a specific date or denomination. Look at each letter and trace a line from letter to letter on the grid. The simpler and more concise you can be, the more specific your intention and the cleaner your design. The resulting pattern becomes your personal sigil. Mark it in the earth or in your container with a trowel and plant the seeds inside the design. Allow the seeds to grow and reach fruition.

Chapter 8

OMENS AND ORACLES: USING HERBS FOR DIVINATION

From reading tea leaves and coffee grounds to recognizing auspicious herbs, traditions of divination from different cultures are plentiful. For example, tea has myriad uses—for prognostication, to drink, and as a ritual or magickal act. The preparation and drinking of tea is an herbal ritual in and of itself. In addition, using tea leaves to predict the future, illuminate a present situation, or discern the energies surrounding an individual or their situation is an enjoyable and enlightening endeavor. A warm beverage and an attentive friend are valuable experiences. Learn about how to interpret the herbs and grounds in your teacup and how to develop and share warmth as well as psychic abilities.

TEA AS PROGNOSTICATION

Tea is the second-most popular beverage in the world, coming in behind water (the sustainer of life itself and an elemental power of emotion and depth). The tea plant, *Camellia sinensis*, has been used for medicinal as well as prophetic purposes. High in polyphenols, which are powerful antioxidants, tea has been used to treat respiratory problems, headaches, coughs and cold, and a variety of other ailments. Recent studies have implicated tea in the prevention of heart disease and cancer. Beverages such as coffee, black tea, and herbal tea are all actually tea, because the word "tea" has also come to refer to the manner in which a warm, herbal beverage is made; however, "tea" is not just a process; it is a specific plant. *Camellia sinensis*, while caffeinated, does not have as sharp a flavor as coffee, nor does it have as much caffeine. *Camellia sinensis* does not linger on the palate like coffee does. Coffee can affect the quality and odor of breath, while tea does not.

The health benefits of consuming tea are numerous, but tea has many different facets to its allure. Once upon a time, tea was rare and expensive and thus difficult to obtain. For this reason, its use was reserved primarily for medicinal purposes. Cultivated in Sri Lanka, India, and Indonesia, the wildcrafted tea plant can grow up to 30 feet tall; however, tea growers usually trim the tea plant to no more than 5 feet in order to facilitate cultivation and harvesting.

During the Victorian era, occultism, secret societies, and a fascination with esoteric energies flourished, and reading tea leaves became a popular method of divination. Before you begin reading tea leaves as a prognosticator for your queries, it is worth considering the different types of tea you might choose. You'll want to make this choice with intention, because each preparation has its own energetic signature.

Black Tea

Black tea is energetically aligned with the ancient crone of wisdom, the waning moon, and the spirits of those beyond the veil. If you are seeking wisdom from beyond, messages from beloveds beyond the veil, or if you are preparing a New Moon ritual, then black tea would be your tea of choice. Black tea is allowed to wither under the sun and ferment, where its color darkens and inspires its name. The tenderness of green is gone but made even more powerful through the solar energies and the energy of death. Witches do not fear death so much as they see it as a transmutation of the spirit. All things proceed from the goddess and all will return to her. Using black tea for divination is powerful.

Green Tea

Green tea is made from the fresh leaves of *Camellia sinensis* and carries with it the spirit of optimism and health. If you wish to consult the tea as an oracle for situations involving change, growth, or emerging from old patterns and establishing the new, green tea would make a good choice. Perhaps you want information about a move you are planning to make, or you are facing some other kind of decision. Green tea will add an energetic alignment to divination on points of change.

Moroccan Tea

Moroccan tea is prepared by making an infusion of green tea and pouring it over a portion of freshly chopped mint. Moroccan tea is an excellent choice of prognosticators who are seeking insight and information into matters of money and fortune. For example, if you wish to use divination in order to ascertain the influence surrounding a change of job or career, Moroccan tea would be an appropriate choice.

First and Second Flush

First flush tea refers not to a variety but rather to the time of year when the tea is harvested. In a first flush tea, the new spring leaves are gathered early in the season. This is the tea of the maiden spirit, used in consultation for indicators of love. If you are seeking information on romantic energies and the possibility of love, first flush green tea would be your tea of choice. The taste of first flush is both gentle and light.

Second flush is used for divination on the energies of established relationships. Because it is more mature and gathered in the fullness of summer, second flush represents the mother aspect. Second flush can be used when divining and meditating on deep relationships, established, long term, or familial.

Oolong

Oolong tea is sort of a blend or hybrid. Oolong is made by allowing green tea leaves to ferment only slightly. This partial fermentation aligns oolong with mixed states. For example, if you are at a crossroads or are attempting to divine a path between two clear choices, oolong would make an appropriate indicator. Additionally, if you are seeking more clarity or just another opinion if the Chariot or the Tower keep turning up in your tarot spreads, oolong is the tea to prepare.

HERBAL TEA AND TASSEOMANCY

Remember that you can create your own tonic tea blend using any of the abovementioned preparations and then amplifying them with herbs that will attune with your reason for seeking communion with an oracle. In tasseomancy, the magickal power of elemental energies (earth and air represented by the herbs, water from the kettle, and the fire that heats the water) can be increased by applying your herbal knowledge and selecting appropriate herbs to craft a custom blend that will align with your purpose. For example, if your question is related to past memories, adding rosemary would be appropriate. Similarly, adding rose would amplify divinations for love, and mint for luck and fortune. Preparation is key, as you will need to use a loose tea that is chopped but not overly processed.

For More on Tasseomancy

The most-often cited reference for tea reading symbols comes from an author known as "A Highland Seer" who created what many consider to be an authentic guide on the interpretation of symbols that was written in 1881. *Reading Tea Leaves* provides a comprehensive and useful guide to symbolic tasseomancy.

Tasseomancy is highly intuitive and requires a strong command of symbolic associations. There are five common types of symbols, and they are fairly self-explanatory. You can expect to see:

- Numbers
- Letters
- Specific objects
- Identifiable animals
- Mythical creatures or beings

Not only are the symbols themselves very important in prognosticating; the placement of where they appear on the cup is paramount as well, as different locations signify different things. Some positions of power and their associations include:

- **The rim of the teacup:** The rim represents the present moment or the questioner's current frame of reality.
- **The sides of the teacup:** This is the sphere of influence that lies just in front of the question; the near future that is just about to come to pass.
- **The bottom of the cup:** This is the distant future, the outcome that will take time to materialize and will be impacted by the actions that the questioner takes or does not take.
- **The handle of the teacup:** The handle is the questioner's current environment, the circumstances under which he or she is presently living and working.

The Modern Witchcraft Guide to Magickal Herbs

The diviner will prepare the tea and the questioner will drink the tea in a meditative state, allowing a clear and specific question to form in their mind. Some diviners will prefer to know the question, but it is not necessary for the questioner to divulge the query. The diviner is interacting with source energy expressed through the herbs on a spiritual level, and truth will come out regardless of the level of communication between the diviner and the questioner. Some questioners who desire a more in-depth reading would be wise to divulge their query, as the diviner will be more able to interpret the symbols in addition to identifying the significance of their placement and appearance as well as their associated meanings.

Reading tea leaves gives you as a practitioner the opportunity to hone your psychic instincts and symbolic knowledge. It also gives you a forum to develop your connection to herbs as well as your interpretation and communication skills. As a questioner, tasseomancy gives you space to meditate on, receive insight about, and reflect upon outcomes that may or may not be predetermined.

PREDICTING AND GROUNDING WITH COFFEE GROUNDS

Reading coffee grounds is a popular practice in Turkey. Turkish coffee is very thick and contains a fair amount of sediment, which makes it a fascinating canvas for prognostication and interpretation. Believed to have begun during the 1600s, the practice of reading coffee grounds extends across the Middle East.

There is no particular type of coffee that is specific to reading grounds; however, the preparation is crucial. The coffee must be made with the finest Turkish powder. Note that "finest" refers not necessarily to the quality of the coffee but to the degree to which it is ground. The powdered grounds and sugar, if desired, are placed in a small, usually copper, Turkish coffee pot and the pot is filled with water. The grounds are boiled over a medium heat until a foam accumulates on top, usually in less than 5 minutes. The foam is then spooned into a white cup while the grounds are boiled for a few seconds longer, then poured over the foam. The questioner drinks the coffee, then places a saucer on top of the rim of the cup. The cup is then vigorously swirled around three times and quickly set upside down on the saucer and allowed to rest for around 10 minutes. The diviner will then look for symbols in the grounds much in the same way that tea leaves are read.

The location of symbols on the cup has significance,too. As in reading tea leaves, where a symbol chooses to manifest is to be taken note of. The cup is divided into expressions of time and tone along a north–south axis and an east–west axis. The cup quadrants and their corresponding energies are as follows:

- North: Negative influence
- South: Positive influence
- East: Near future
- West: Distant future

Attention is paid not only to the type and location of the symbols but also to their size. Both the cup and the saucer are read, with the cup representing the questioner's surrounding environment such as employment, commerce, and labor, while the saucer represents the questioner's private or home life and matters of the heart. Symbols are sought in the sediment while taking into account their general distribution throughout the cup, the intensity of their color, as well as any significant shapes or trails.

Chapter 9

BELLADONNA AND BANES: HERBAL EXPLORATIONS OF LIGHTS AND SHADOWS

lso known as deadly nightshade, belladonna has a long and storied history. In this chapter, you'll learn which night-flowering
herbs to use and which to avoid and the properties of powerful
herbs used in spells and charms designed to remove obstacles, overcome adversity, address wrongdoings, and confront inequity. Because
so many are poisonous, you won't find many spells or rituals in this
chapter, but since these herbs are prominently associated with witchcraft, they are very important to know.

BELLADONNA, THE BANE

Some herbs are poisonous. Nonetheless, they feature prominently in
witchcraft. While they should not be handled or ingested, they should
also be known and understood.

Atropa bella-donna is one such herb. Also known as deadly nightshade, it was aptly named by the naturalist Carolus Linnaeus. Its evocative name brings to mind the fates and the servant of beauty and love.
Belladonna, as it is referred to in Italy, contains atropine. Women from
the southern region of Italy were said to have used a dilution of atropine
in their eyes, causing their pupils to dilate and giving their eyes a
darkly dreamy look that was alluring to members of the opposite sex.

John Gerard claimed that women also used belladonna to impart a paleness to their cheeks, while others maintained that the dark and glossy berries were used for the opposite effect. Women purportedly stained their cheeks with the reddish-purple juice of the shiny black belladonna fruit. The herb came to be strongly associated with seductive beauty, beautiful women, wise women, and witches. The truth is that all parts of the belladonna plant are poisonous. The berries are attractive and sweet but sometimes fatal when eaten.

HEMLOCK

A poison cup of hemlock mixed with wine dispatched one of the greatest philosophers ever known to history. Socrates succumbed to the drink laced with hemlock in 399 B.C.E., as this was a common method of execution for criminals at the time. Accused of "corrupting the young" along with another charge of "impiety," the condemnation to death and its subsequent administration deprived the world of one of its most innovative thinkers.

Hemlock had other uses besides the death penalty. Dioscorides wrote that a poultice of hemlock applied to a man's testicles would discourage promiscuity. When applied to a woman's breast, hemlock would interfere with lactation and even puberty by stopping breast growth in sexually immature females. How did this dangerous herb come to be associated with witchcraft?

In ancient Greece, hemlock trees were dedicated to the goddess Hecate. A goddess of the moon and of darkness, Hecate was a protectress of witches. There is no doubt that at one time hemlock was cultivated in monastic gardens. Because of its libido-killing properties, it was considered important to those who wished above all else to live a chaste life.

Hemlock is included among the ingredients of the mysterious and famed witch's flying ointment. While some witches would use hemlock as chicken feed, intoxicating the chickens and thus making them easier to steal, others used it as a topical salve. It is said that a small application of water hemlock and poison hemlock containing coniine, a volatile and poisonous compound, imparts a sensation that is likened to gliding through the air. Poisonous, emasculating, and mind-altering, the power of hemlock is nothing to be trifled with.

MANDRAKE: OF MANDRAGORA AND MAYAPPLE

Few herbs command mythology and mystery quite like mandrake. Its anthropomorphic form caused fascination and obsession around this herb. Pythagoras imagined that the taproot could possibly be a tiny human, or, alternately, a doll.

Mandrake was ascribed dangerous powers. Flavius Josephus, a Roman historian, general, and diplomat, claimed that mandrake emitted an eerie red glow at night. The plant was said to move of its own free will and that in order to get close to it, someone had to immobilize the plant with a bath of urine mixed with menstrual blood. Removing the herb from the ground could only be done with assistance. It was believed that only a dog could uproot the mandrake, but in so doing, the dog would surely die. As time passed, the mystique of the mandrake only grew. Aelian suggested that the plant was altogether invisible by daylight because it possessed the power to conceal itself among other plants.

The resemblance of its taproot to the human form caused a sinister air to gather around mandrake. The mandrake was thought to be one of the creator God's "first drafts" as he conceived the manifestation of Adam, whom he would later build from clay. The plant was considered rare because it was believed to grow only near the Garden of Eden. Mandrake did, however, grow in morbid places. Mandrake was thought to favor the land beneath the gallows, sprouting up where the fluids of the doomed came into contact with the earth.

People were terrified of mandrake—but some were more than willing to pay for it. Rare and expensive, mandrake was believed to make its owner invincible in battle and irresistible to women. Owning a mandrake was to own good health and riches, but only if it was properly handled. Superstition required that a mandrake had to be bathed in wine and dressed in silk, even fed. Mandrake was believed to have the power to produce the philosopher's stone, a talisman that could bestow immortality. If the mandrake did not perform any of its ascribed tasks, it was assumed that the cause was disinterest or boredom with its owner. Unfortunately, a mandrake could not be easily disposed of. Giving it away was forbidden, as was reselling for less than the original price. Oftentimes, owners were buried with their mandrakes.

Just when mandrake fever had reached its height, its mystique began to unravel. In 1597, John Gerard was among the first to disavow the powers ascribed to mandrake by digging one up himself, following on the heels of William Turner, who claimed in 1551 that the root didn't really look much like a human at all.

While centuries have passed since the time it was believed that the fatal screams of the mandrake would kill anyone within earshot, it is worth noting that all parts of the plant are indeed poisonous. This is one characteristic that *Mandragora officinarum* shares with *Podophyllum peltatum*. Known as mayapple, *Podophyllum peltatum* is often referred to by the misnomer "American mandrake." This small, perennial herb has a thin, creeping rhizome that bears no resemblance to mandragora. Included in the *British Pharmacopoeia*, the plant was known to Native Americans and was used as a vermifuge as well as an emetic.

More on Mayapple

Another name for mayapple is duck's foot, which is a reference to the shape of its leaves. American mandrake is part of the barberry family and has nothing at all to do with the legendary mandragora, which was so thoroughly feared.

THE WITCH'S FLYING OINTMENT

What then, do belladonna, hemlock, and mandrake all have in common? They are all cited as ingredients in the storied witch's flying ointment. Some believed that witches had the ability to transform themselves into winged creatures such as owls. There are many descriptions of witch's flying ointment, recorded in the 1500s and 1600s, and some truly horrific ingredients are mentioned. Plants that are most frequently cited in witch's flying ointment include:

- Water hemlock
- Hemlock
- Celery
- Sweet flag
- Yellow flag
- Water lily
- Creeping cinquefoil
- Tormentil
- Monkshood
- Poppy
- Deadly nightshade
- Henbane
- Black nightshade
- Mandrake
- Thorn apple
- Spurge
- Darnel
- Lettuce
- Purslane
- Poplar
- Oil (unspecified)
- Incense (unspecified)
- Soot

The Modern Witchcraft Guide to Magickal Herbs

The animal ingredients are not worth mentioning because they are taboo. Not only that, but they do not include any ascribed power other than shock value. Including them in an herbal serves no purpose.

PERSEPHONE'S REALM: DARKNESS AND AGRICULTURAL SEASONS

The Middle Ages were not the first time that the pursuit of herbs and plants had serious repercussions. Classical Greek mythology explains the agricultural cycle of seasons as the by-product of an abduction. At the time of her abduction, Persephone was said to have been gathering violets. So enamored of the maiden goddess, daughter of Demeter the earth mother, was Hades that he split the earth and arose from the underworld, capturing the maiden and making her his queen. This sent Demeter into a state of despair and set the cycle of seasons into motion. So great was the grief of the divine mother that she laid waste to all plant life on earth. So great was the destruction that Zeus, ruler of the gods and goddesses of Olympus, intervened and petitioned Hades for Persephone's return.

Because she had eaten the seeds of a pomegranate while she was in the underworld (not knowing that they would bind her to the realm of darkness), Persephone was only permitted to reunite with her mother for seven months of the year. The rest of the time, she would rule in darkness as queen of the damned, her fate set into motion by violets and sealed by the seeds of the pomegranate. In mythology, we understand the powerful and important role that the plants will play, their presence affecting the outcome of all life on earth. As we attempt to make sense of the changing world, we are reminded of the power of darkness and its place in magick.

HOW TO SAFELY USE CERTAIN HERBS OF DARKNESS

Without darkness, there is no light. How do the nocturnal plants know that their pale white glow will attract moths to their blossoms, ensuring the survival of their species as they are pollinated through the attraction of delicate winged creatures of the night? What divine perfection and consciousness is present in a wandering vine that knows how to exhibit just the right shimmering shade? And how can you harness this alluring and cunning beauty to enhance your modern practice of magick?

Night Blooming Living Altar Craft

We all have our distinct circadian rhythms. Some witches rise with the rosy-fingered goddess of the dawn as she rises and illuminates the sky. Others find comfort in the darkness. Many children grow up with a fear of the dark, while others embrace it, finding solace in the shadows and a connection with the creatures of the night. Cats and owls in particular resonate with many witches, and while herbal magick is strongly connected to the sun, there is also much beauty to be beheld only by moonlight.

Evening primrose releases the dulcet aroma of its pale petal-pink flowers at dusk. For those who are just coming alive during the golden hour when day succumbs to night, growing evening primrose is an effective way to experience the beauty of between the worlds. Moonflower, as its name suggests, is another flower that blooms at night, its delicate white flowers releasing a slightly citrus scent. White as the moon, aromatic and bright, a vine of moonflower near your altar will add contemplative beauty to your sacred space only at night, for the blossoms fade by morning. Other flowering plants that open at night include night phlox, evening stock, and angel's trumpet.

On your windowsill, you can create a living nocturnal altar by placing a window planter with one of the climbing plants mentioned, such as moonflower (*Ipomoea alba*). You will need:

- About 18 feet jute twine
- Small plastic hula hoop with a diameter of about 1 yard
- Suction cup with hook

1. Tie the twine to the topmost centered point on the hula hoop and run it down diagonally to the spot between seven and eight o'clock. Loop it around the hula hoop and pull the long end of the twine through the loop, pulling it tightly. Run it over to the three o'clock spot and repeat the loop, thread through the loop, and tighten process. Run the twine across to the nine o'clock spot and repeat. Continue to the lower right between four and five o'clock, making the tie-off and finishing back at the top to create a giant 3-foot pentacle armature inside of the hoop.

2. Using a suction cup with hook, hang the pentagram armature in your window above the window box. As the moonflower grows, it will seek out the armature and grow around it. As evening falls, the

ghostly white blooms will open before your eyes. They will remain open until morning, keeping you company throughout the night.

3. The pentacle will also cast a protective charm over your home. No one is going to break into a house with a giant night-blooming pentagram glowing in the window (especially if you invert it). You can also recite a protective charm to enhance its powers, especially if you are feeling unsafe:

> "May this pentagram protect
> May this dwelling be blessed
> That all who dwell and enter here
> Shall do so in the absence of fear."

COUNTER CRAFT TO STOP DARKNESS

Witches are notorious for throwing shade. If you feel that you have been the recipient of unwanted energy, you may wish to engage in counter craft. Counter craft has a long and storied history, and although it is shrouded in secrecy, many otherwise unexplainable artifacts remain. Discoveries of counter craft include magickal objects hidden inside houses. These objects may be any number of apotropaic charms, including mummified or other feline remains, a single shoe, a horseshoe, skulls of animals (particularly horses), as well as sigils and other ritualistic markings.

Witch Bottles

Witch bottles are an effective type of counter magick and lend themselves easily to incorporating appropriate herbal ingredients. A witch bottle can be made as a ward and then hidden in your house or hidden in the house of the person from whom you believe the unwanted energy originated. Be sure to use an opaque bottle in order to conceal the contents of the bottle so that they are not readily discovered. If you don't have an opaque bottle, you can wash and paint the outside of an empty spice bottle. To create a witch bottle, you will need:

- Herbs and materials based on your needs:
  - If you are seeking to break a cycle of scarcity, you would include coins, metallic objects such as a gold four-leaf clover, and dried herbs from the mint family.

- If you wanted to improve your psychic abilities in order to gain information or insight about a person or situation, you would include a quartz crystal for mental clarity, salt, and fennel seeds.
- If you wanted to heal a rift between lovers, you would take a piece of ripped red felt and sew it together, placing it in the bottle, needle and all, with rose quartz and rosebuds.
- A dark glass bottle of cobalt or amber or of an opaque material such as clay (bottle should have lid and wax for sealing)

1. Add the herbs or materials to the bottle and seal the lid or cork permanently with wax and place your bottle in a secret location.
2. As you place the bottle, give it specific instructions, such as:

> "SACRED MAGICK
> SECRET CHARM
> UNDISCOVERED
> DO NO HARM
> PLACED WITH POWER
> SUBTLE YET STRONG
> UPON MY HAND
> WILL COME NO WRONG.
> BY ALL THE POWER
> OF THREE TIMES THREE
> AS I WILL
> SO MUST IT BE."

3. Set your intention from a place of positivity, and your witch bottles will work their magick in craftiness and in darkness.

Herbal Spell to Stop Gossip

This spell is intended to aid the witch in putting an end to false gossip. It begins on the dark moon. You will need:
- Mortar and pestle
- Fresh rosemary needles
- 3 ginkgo leaves
- 3 mugwort leaves
- Bolline (the white-handled knife used for practical magickal workings)
- Large or small (see directions) fresh aloe vera leaf
- Small bowl

- Small glass jar or witch bottle with a wide opening, such as a small jelly jar sampler
- 1–2 teaspoons clove buds
- Dash of cayenne pepper
- Beeswax candle

1. Bring your tools and ingredients to your altar. Lay them out and bless them with a charge as you set your intention and visualize your target:

> "I COME TO THE ALTAR OF POWER
> TO PUT A HALT TO GOSSIP.
> THE SOURCE WILL BE SILENCED.
> THE RECIPIENT WILL BE VINDICATED.
> THE TRUTH SHALL BECOME KNOWN."

2. In your mortar and pestle, gently macerate the rosemary, then add the ginkgo and mugwort leaves. In this spell, the mugwort represents psychic ability, rosemary is for the memory of the negative false and hurtful words, and ginkgo is the amplifier. As the herbs are combined and transformed, take in their aroma. Crushing the rosemary transforms the memory of what has been said. Combining it with mugwort sets your intention, and the ginkgo lends it power.

3. Next, take your bolline and split the aloe leaf. When you choose the leaf, make sure it is the right size. The size of the leaf will be determined by the size of the problem. If the gossip has gotten out of hand, choose a large leaf. If the problem is still in the early stages, a small leaf can be used to nip it in the bud. Scoop out the mucilage into a small bowl and add the macerated herbs, stirring them in with your finger sunwise. The aloe vera represents truth, and by combining these four ingredients, the right energy is activated. Transfer the potion into the jar and keep it with you. Use it for anointing any area you encounter in which the gossip has spread, including the space or personal effects of the perpetrator. Some examples include placing a drop on a phone case, a desk, a computer keyboard, or a pen or notebook.

4. Finally, you will take the outer hollowed-out leaf of the aloe and do some corrective spellcasting to prevent any more gossip. Fill it with clove buds and a sprinkling of cayenne and put the halves

back together. This represents "nipping it in the bud" so that it does not continue. Light the beeswax candle and use the molten wax to seal the leaf closed so that the buds and pepper are trapped inside and nothing more can get out. You can even use the aloe to smooth over the serrated edges of the leaf in a bit of sympathetic magick, which will help heal the relationship between you and the perpetrator.

5. Leave the charm to dry thoroughly as the moon waxes. When the moon is full, you can complete the spell by burning the charm entirely in your cauldron. Gather and bury the ashes. So must it be done.

Chapter 10

DRAGON'S BLOOD AND DREAMS: USING HERBS FOR PSYCHIC AND SPIRITUAL HEALING

Resins and aromatic herbs can heal the psyche and spirit and have anti-inflammatory properties as well. In this chapter, you'll learn about herbal incense blends as dreamy teas and tonics, spells, and charms for the mind using herbs.

DRAGON'S BLOOD

Sometimes a sinister-sounding herb does not quite live up to its name. The dragon is a polarized mythological creature. In the Eastern tradition, the dragon is a symbol of regenerative power and wisdom. The dragon is revered and not feared. In Western culture, the dragon guards the hoard of gold and must be appeased with the sacrifice of a woman. To conquer the dragon is to free the flow of fertility and abundance: Rescue the maiden and claim the treasure. Defeating the dragon was to bring glory. How do we reconcile such diametrically opposed interpretations of powerful symbolism, and how do herbs factor into this dichotomy?

Just as belladonna sounds lovely but isn't, dragon's blood sounds frightening but is actually beneficial. Also known as *sangre de drago*, the Latin binomial for dragon's blood is *Croton lechleri*. This flowering plant is native to South America and is credited with several ethnomedicinal uses. The resinous sap is used to treat maladies that range from diarrhea to insect bites and inflammations. The dark red sap appears to have powers that are just beginning to be understood. Laboratory studies have demonstrated that dragon's blood even has the potential to kill cancer cells. In clinical trials, it has been shown to ease AIDS-related diarrhea. Studies done on animals indicate that dragon's blood can decrease the amount of time it takes for a wound to heal.

In magick, dragon's blood is used as an incense, an ingredient in spells and charms, and even a color additive for ink used to write in witches' grimoires. Artificial dragon's blood and dragon's blood ink is frequently sold but has nothing to do with the red resinous healing sap that is true dragon's blood. Still it is important to be both studious and discerning, as herbs with attractive-sounding names, like belladonna, are incredibly dangerous, while ominous-sounding herbs, like dragon's blood, possess some authentic healing properties along with low toxicity. Knowledge and safety are paramount when working with herbs. Herbs are capable of tremendous healing capacity, including healing the spirit. There are many activities for which you can use dragon's blood:

- Crush 1 tablespoon of the dried resin and combine it with ½ cup of Epsom salts and ¼ cup sea salt and dissolve in your bathwater to create a dragon's blood bath.
- Combine dragon's blood resin with copal in a mortar and pestle and crush into a powder. (You might need to use a hammer first in order to break up the larger pieces.) The powder can be burned like incense on a charcoal in a fireproof container such as a cauldron.
- Add whole pieces of dragon's blood to a sachet or mojo bag and carry it around with you.

HERBS FOR RELAXATION AND DREAMS

Herbs such as skullcap, mugwort, valerian, and hypericum or St. John's wort have all been ascribed with healing powers. Although definitive clinical trials are somewhat lacking, there is little doubt that powerful herbs such as valerian have helped people achieve a better night's sleep. Hypericum has been documented to combat the effects of mild depression, while skullcap and mugwort are said to have enhanced clairvoyant abilities in those who use them for this purpose.

It is possible to get the benefit of healing herbs without ingesting them. Allergies can develop late in life, and one cannot be too careful when researching herbs and studying their potential for side effects. Luckily, there are no side effects to creating a dream pillow. And infusing it with herbs gives you a perfectly safe way to enjoy some of the healing properties that herbs contain. To make a basic dream pillow, you will need:

- A 10" × 9" piece of natural fabric such as cotton or silk
- Needle and thread
- 1 cup flax seeds
- ½ cup aromatic dried herbs such as lavender, rosemary, lemon balm, mint, or a combination using several of those mentioned

1. Fold the cloth in half to make a 5" × 9"-long pocket. Sew up two sides, leaving one side open.
2. Fill the pocket with the flax seeds and then add the herbs. Continue sewing until the pocket is sealed.
3. You can sleep with the pillow across your eyes or put it under your neck or next to you on your pillow so that you can breathe in its scent. This will promote relaxation and a sense of peace.

Chapter 11

RITES AND RITUALS: MAGICKAL AND RITUAL USE OF HERBS

Witches follow a cycle of seasons in their celebrations. The witch's New Year begins at Samhain, the cross-quarter sabbat that heralds the dead and the approach of winter. This is the time when herbs shift their energetic resources from leaf to root. Traditionally associated with honoring the dead, Samhain is also a time for growth, as this is the time when the seed is revealed. The seed will fall to earth or be scattered by the wind, whereupon it will nestle in the damp earth and sleep through the long dark of winter to be reborn as Ostara approaches. Growing to maturity at Beltane and reaching the height of potency at Litha, herbs will explode in blossom and leaf, connecting us to the cycle of the seasons. As we progress through the harvest time, we witness the sacred cycle of the Wheel of the Year embodied by the life cycle of our herbal partners in magick. As such, witches approach the gathering, harvest, and storage of herbs in a ritual fashion. In this chapter, we will learn how to ritually gather herbs, as well as which herbs are in season and how they can be incorporated into the traditional witch's sabbats.

THE GATHERING

There are many traditions and superstitions surrounding the gathering of herbs. Since witchcraft is primarily an anecdotal tradition, passed down from priestesses to initiates, apart from highly secretive grimoires and books of shadows, it is difficult to separate tradition from lore. Some elements of folklore have become traditions because modern witches have revived their practice. Such is the case with modern-day druids and other neo-pagans. Seeking to imbue a modern practice with the significance of time and tradition, activities attributed to ancient practices have renewed value. Gathering herbs can be approached as a ritual endeavor, and this is supported through the folklore ascribed to the ancient druids.

Just as you ritually prepare magickal tools for spellcraft at your altar, this same care should be afforded to the tools with which you gather. Before setting out for a forage or a trip to the market, first take some time to enter ritual space and set your intention. Envision the highest possible outcomes from the herbs you seek. Which ones will you use for wellness? What health aspects do you need to address right now? If you have charms or spells in mind, think about their purpose. Setting out with a purpose frames your mind to come into alignment with the work at hand. (Remember, do not use tools made of iron, as this is considered a taboo.)

If you plan to forage for wildcrafted herbs, you will need:

- Illustrated botanical reference for identification
- Bolline (the white-handled knife used for practical magickal workings)
- Small scythe (also a ritual tool)
- Garden snips or small handheld shears
- Trowel or root digger
- Basket or small brown paper bags

1. It is customary to dress in white when gathering herbs, and some witches will even venture out barefoot. To walk barefoot upon the earth (also known as "grounding") is to experience every root, rock, and acorn, every bladed leaf. To feel the earth gently give under the weight of your step brings you close to divine energy. If you are highly sensitive and cannot bear to walk barefoot upon

the earth, at least take off your shoes and stand still, coming into direct physical skin contact with the Great Mother and keeper and nurturer of your sacred herbs for at least a few minutes. This act of attunement is done with humility and respect. Even a few minutes of standing barefoot upon the earth can reset your electromagnetic field and establish a magickal connection to the sacred work of gathering. Cultivating awareness of this energy exchange will enhance not just your physiological wellness but also the magick of your gathering.

2. Use your illustrated botanical field guide for plant identification. Illustrations are preferable to photographs because photos do not necessarily indicate scale. Additionally, an undesirable photographic angle can lead to misidentification. Once you have correctly identified the herbs you need, meditate on your required quantity. Dried herbs will degrade over time, so there is no point in gathering more than you intend to use within the year. Plan to dry and store how much you will need for tinctures or oil infusions that will have a longer shelf life.

3. Take only what you need. Before you cut them, talk to your herbs. Invite them to be a part of your sacred work.

The Benefits of Grounding

There is a scientifically proven exchange of electrons when we come into direct contact with the earth. Loss of this connection can lead to a host of wellness issues including pain, lethargy, and insomnia. Grounding, or "earthing" as it is also known, can also eliminate free radicals from the body, resulting in improved sleep patterns and reduction of chronic pains.

HERBS FOR EVERY SEASON

For every sabbat and cross-quarter day on the Great Wheel, there is an herbal correspondence. From remembering our ancestors to the quiet contemplation of the solstices to the new growth of sprouts and the beauty of bringing an herbal harvest to the quiet darkness of the cupboard, herbs enrich and enliven the practice of magick. If you want to incorporate herbs in rituals throughout the year, there are many ways to do so. Take a journey through the Wheel of the Year and add aromatic herbs and spices at every step on the path.

Samhain Spices

Would it shock you to learn that pumpkin spice is a bit of a misnomer? Pumpkin is a revered gourd that is made palatable by numerous herbs and spices including cinnamon, clove, ginger, nutmeg, and allspice, among others. These aromatic and intensely flavorful spices have strong associations with autumn, as they are almost exclusively used in a dried state. They have come to represent the dark time of the year when herbs are stored in cool, dark places. Cinnamon and clove have associations with crone goddess energy. They possess an intensity that resonates with her power. Beyond flavoring cookies, cakes, and coffee, these powerful energies can be used for consecration and to bring herbal magick to your practice. The following spice blend can be burned as an incense, added to coffee grounds before percolating, as well as included in recipes. You can also gather the herbs together as an herbal charm. Place a teaspoon on the center of a black cloth and tie with a silver thread to make a meaningful Samhain herbal charm or offering to your ancestors on your Samhain altar. For the blend you will need:

- ¼ teaspoon allspice
- ¼ teaspoon dried ginger
- ⅛ teaspoon dried and ground clove
- ½ teaspoon nutmeg
- ½ teaspoon cinnamon
- Mortar and pestle
- Small pot

Combine all the herbs in your mortar and pestle. Mix them thoroughly then transfer them to keep in a small pot and use to sprinkle a little Samhain magick wherever it is needed.

Wild Sister Silver Broomstick Samhain Tea

Samhain is the witch's New Year. At Samhain, we celebrate both a beginning and an ending. This is also the time of year when the veil between the worlds grows thin and communication with the spirit world is made easier by virtue of the closeness of the earthly realm to the ethereal realm. Witches believe that the spirit world is separated from the mundane world only by a veil that shrouds and protects one world from the adjacent domain. While the altar represents a point of communion between these two worlds, it is generally understood that they remain separate. However, at Samhain, this separation is less pronounced than at other times of the year. By opening the mind to the possibilities of communicating or interacting with the spirit world, we can receive both affirmations and insights about the world we live in as well as the lives we are leading. To facilitate this exchange of energy (you must invest in the exchange by participating and giving of yourself) you can prepare and share an inspired herbal tea that embodies the energy of the season. The ingredients are simple and relatively easy to obtain, and the presentation is delightful and worthy of a sabbat or solitary observance. You will need:

- Handful of freshly gathered mugwort leaves
- Kitchen scissors
- Natural cotton chef-grade cooking twine
- Cinnamon stick for every participant
- Small silver broom
- Kettle, teacups, and saucers

1. Gently trim the mugwort leaves from the stalk with kitchen scissors, leaving a small amount of leaf stem. Lay them out silver-side up so that you can judge their size. Choose around eight leaves that are approximately the same length and gather them together.
2. Cut 1 foot of twine. Take a cinnamon stick and position it in the center of the bundle with ½ inch of the stick covered by the leaf stems. Find the center point of the twine and wrap it 3 times around the outside of the mugwort leaves. Tie a tight half knot and flip the mugwort and cinnamon bouquet over. Tie another half knot on the opposite side of the bouquet. Continue tying half knots on opposite sides, working your way slowly up the stick until the leaf stems are completely covered.
3. When the leaf stems are covered, tie a very tight knot and then finish the bouquet with a bow knot. Trim any excess twine. Put the kettle on and allow the water to boil. Place the tiny silver broomstick in a teacup and pour the boiled water over it, allowing it to steep until the water is cool.
4. Clear your mind of your earthly cares and allow your third eye to open and your psychic abilities to become accessible. As you sip the tea, allow your spirit to soar and greet your beloved, who have passed beyond the veil. The silver broom becomes the conduit

of travel beyond the limits of sensory perception. Allow yourself to send and receive messages. Accept any messages received or insights gained as evidence of the efficacy of the herbal spell.

5. Mugwort and cinnamon have associations with the maiden and crone aspects of the goddess. You are acting as the mother, the one who brings these two worlds together, the beginning and the ending into the now to complete the threefold manifestation of magick. Sip your tea, relax, and enjoy the possibilities of sharing a magickal experience during a sacred time.

The Herbs of Yule: Evergreens, Pomanders, and Mistletoe

The traditions and trappings that surround the solar return are some of the most enduring and beloved of modern observances in witchcraft. The scent of pine in the home evokes feelings of warmth, of gatherings, goodwill, and familial love. Using evergreens such as fir and pine brings an earthy scent and a comforting vibe to your home. The needles can be displayed along with pine cones as a potpourri and dusted with a finely crushed mix of frankincense and myrrh resins. Alternately, you can gather small branches and layer them over a circular armature such as a large embroidery hoop, affixing them to the hoop with green floral tape. You can also create your own wreath by creating an armature out of 8-gauge wire, bent in a circle of the diameter of your choice and covered with evergreen boughs. Add a sprig of mistletoe and a brightly colored ribbon to create a festive symbol of the unbroken circle.

Another way to incorporate herbs at Yule is to make an orange and clove pomander. These are aromatic, attractive, and easy to create. You will need:

- Toothpick
- Orange
- Handfuls of dried whole clove buds
- Wire cutters
- Floral wire
- Ribbon
- Pliers
- Brown paper bag (optional)

1. Using the toothpick, make small perforations in the skin of the orange. Be creative and magickal, using your occult knowledge to create sigils and star patterns, elemental and planetary symbols. In each perforation, place the stem of a clove bud and press it into the orange.
2. Use the wire cutters to cut a length of floral wire and run it through the orange, leaving ½ an inch of wire exposed through the bottom. Make a loop at the top and run the wire back down through the orange. Twist the ends of the wire together at the bottom and conceal by tying a decorative ribbon around the twisted wire or by bending it up with the pliers and tucking it into the fruit. The pomander will smell wonderful and look enchanting. You can also put the orange in a paper bag to dry out so it will last longer.

Imbolc Incense: Herbs of Rebirth

Imbolc is the time of quickening. It is the first light in the dark of winter and is often celebrated with candlelight. Adding a special incense adds magick to Imbolc, as this is a time of initiation. You will need:

- Copal resin
- Petals from dried white roses (white roses are considered sacred to the Celtic goddess Brighid, who is celebrated on Imbolc)
- Bay laurel
- Myrrh
- Small cauldron with heatproof trivet
- Charcoal round

1. Grind the copal resin, rose petals, and laurel and myrrh together. Place a small cauldron on a heatproof trivet and light a charcoal round. When the coal turns gray, sprinkle a little of your incense mix onto the coal and enjoy the scent.
2. The incense can be used for invoking the element of air and the direction of east to call in new beginnings at the start of an Imbolc ritual or as a solitary offering to a serene and beautiful point of change. Any time you use your Imbolc incense, you can recite the following incantation:

> "DAUGHTER OF SUNRISE
> SHINING WOMAN
> MOTHER OF THE FORGE

HEALER OF ALL WOUNDS
FIRST LIGHT IN THE DARK OF WINTER
THE QUICKENING IN THE WOMB
THE DEPTHS OF THE WELL
YOURS IS THE FIRE OF THE HEART
THE FIRE OF HEALING
YOURS IS THE FIRE OF THE TORCH
THE FIRE OF INSPIRATION
YOURS IS THE POETIC MIND
THE POWER OF THE WORD
FROM YOUR WELLS OF INSPIRATION
BEAUTY AND CREATIVITY FLOW
BELOVED AND HONORED
BLESSED BY YOUR NAME.
HAIL, BRIGHID!"

Consecrated Candles for Candlemas

Incorporating herbs into candle magick is satisfying and easy. Since Candlemas is celebrated as the first light in the dark of winter, creating and lighting pillar candles is a magickal ritual in and of itself. You will need:

- Honeycomb beeswax candle sheet
- Hair dryer
- Cotton string for wicks
- Essential oil of rose
- Selection of Imbolc herbs such as basil, coltsfoot, snowdrops, or tansy

1. Before you begin, bless all of your magickal ingredients with a spoken charm such as:
   "BLESSED BE THE BEE
   BLESSED BE THE COTTON
   BLESSED BE THE HERBS
   BURNED BUT NOT FORGOTTEN
   BLESSED BE THE LIGHT
   AND THE WHEEL AS IT TURNS
   BLESSED BE THE CANDLES
   AND THE LOVE WITH WHICH THEY BURN."

2. Lay the beeswax sheet on a clean flat surface. Allow the wax to reach room temperature so that it is pliable. Cold wax is likely to break. If the wax is not pliable, turn on the hair dryer on the low setting and use it to slightly heat up the wax, taking great care not to melt it but merely to soften it. Cut an appropriate length of the cotton and impregnate the wick with the rose oil and set it aside. Gently press the herbs into the warmed beeswax sheet.

3. Turn the sheet over and lay the length of the cotton wicking string along one vertical side. Leave ½ an inch of string overlapping and exposed over the edges. Carefully press the string into the wax and roll the wax around the string until it is the desired thickness. The tighter you roll the wax, the better your candle will perform. Take care and go slow so that the roll is as straight as possible until you reach the desired thickness.

4. Trim one end of the wick flush with the bottom and about ¼ inch at the top. Light your herbal candle and bask in its beautiful glow.

Ostara: The Flowers of Springtime

Creating sweet floral waters and using them as elixirs and libations is a delightful way to attune with the lush beauty of spring. A floral water is light and refreshing. It can be used as a refreshment or as part of a ritual. Floral waters should be made in small quantities and used quickly. They are basically diluted herbal preparations and make a lovely floral addition to the rites of spring. This recipe is a variation on one taught by Susun Weed that she learned in New Zealand. You will need:

- Zest of 4 lemons
- Juice of 4 lemons
- 1 rounded teaspoon cream of tartar
- 1¾ cups sugar
- Large glass or plastic container able to hold a gallon of liquid
- 1 cup fresh violet blossoms
- 1 cup elder blossoms
- 1 gallon spring water

1. Combine the zest, lemon juice, cream of tartar, and sugar in a large container. Pour the gallon of spring water into the container. Add the fresh flowers, cover loosely, and allow them to steep for at least 24 hours.

2. Strain out the flowers after a full day and allow the elixir to rest for a week and then enjoy.

Hawthorn, the Harbinger of Beltane

Hawthorn berries are the fruits of spring. The first flowers of the hawthorn signal the arrival of Beltane, and the fruits that follow mark the culmination of the season. This essence of Beltane can be captured in a potion and enlivened with a charm. To create Beltane Brandy, you will need:

- Brandy
- Hawthorn berries, enough to fill a jar only halfway
- Glass jar with tight-fitting lid

1. Pour brandy over the berries, ensuring that they are completely covered. Seal the jar tightly and keep it in a cool and dark place. Shake the jar daily and as you do so light a candle while reciting the incantation:

  "SACRED BELTANE FIRES BURN
  LIGHT THE WAY FOR SPRING'S RETURN
  WINTER'S DARKNESS NOW MUST END
  THE GREAT WHEEL OF LIFE HAS TURNED AGAIN."

2. Let the potion steep for a month, taking care to leave it outside under the full moon. After a full lunation cycle has passed, you can strain out the brandy and compost the berries. Your potion will retain the magick of Beltane and will also have a delightful flavor.

Litha and the Fruits of Midsummer

Create a festive fruit salad worthy of the faerie folk by using in-season herbs and flowers. You will need:

- Basil
- Mint
- Assortment of melon balls: watermelon, honeydew, cantaloupe
- Sliced grapes
- Minced Pink Lady apples
- Juice of 1 lemon
- Maple syrup or honey, optional
- Feta cheese, optional

1. Shred the basil and mint leaves finely and combine them thoroughly, then set aside.

2. Assemble a compote with melon balls of watermelon, honeydew, and cantaloupe. Add grapes and apples. Spritz with the juice of 1 lemon and toss with the minced herbs.

3. Drizzle with honey or maple syrup and top with a light crumble of feta cheese, if desired. Share with your midsummer companions and enjoy!

Lughnasadh and Sacred Grains

Oats and barley are highly nutritive grains, and Lughnasadh is a perfect time to partake of them as repast. You can start by making barley water by boiling 1 cup barley in 4 cups water until the pearls are tender. Strain and retain the liquid and use it to make an oat-straw infusion in the barley water, adding an ounce of oatstraw. Steep with fresh peppermint and add honey to taste. Enjoy a warm cup of healthy grains as summer recedes into fall.

Mabon and the Bounty of Harvest

Mabon is a perfect time to partake of roasted roots. Choose from a variety of roots such as sweet potatoes or yams, beets, carrots, parsnips, and white potatoes. You can even use all of these roots in one dish. You will need:

- Selected roots, sliced and chopped
- ¼ cup olive oil
- Needles from a sprig of fresh rosemary
- 1 clove garlic, minced
- ¼ teaspoon sea salt
- Orange slices with rind

1. In a medium bowl, toss the roots with the oil, rosemary, garlic, and salt so that everything is evenly coated. Line a baking pan with a sheet of parchment paper and spread the coated roots out in a single layer. Top with a few thinly sliced orange slices, rind and all.

2. Bake for 20 minutes at 350°F and share with your ritual companions.

Chapter 12

CREATIVE ALTAR CRAFT: INCORPORATING HERBS INTO MAGICKAL TOOLS

From making your own herbal grimoire to expressing your spirituality through a living altar and a magick broom, this chapter delves into herbal altar craft with activities that are infused with herbal magick. Learn how to create your own sacred space by creating smudge sticks based on indigenous American tradition and inspired by modern magick.

HERBARIUM AS AN HERBAL GRIMOIRE

A magickal herbarium is in essence a type of grimoire. It is a record and a journal of your personal experience with herbs. Whether you cultivate your own, wild forage, or purchase fresh herbs, compiling and maintaining an herbarium is a way to capture your knowledge and experience. An herbarium is also a guide. Its purpose is not only to document but also to inform. An herbarium, while delicate, can last for years if handled and maintained properly. An herbarium goes far beyond flower pressing and serves as a permanent record of your empirical experience with your working partners in the herbal world. The herbarium is useful because unlike drawings and photographs, you have actual representations of dried herbal specimens. This project can be done by an individual witch or as a group endeavor to compile the collective knowledge of a coven. You will need different supplies for different parts of the process of creating the herbarium. For the gathering part, you will need:

- Field notebook and pen
- Camera
- Garden snips, scissors, or shears
- Clean sheets of paper
- Heavy book such as an unabridged dictionary, textbook, or telephone book
- Gloves
- Backpack for carrying supplies

1. If you are gathering wildcrafted herbs, you will bring these tools with you out into nature and gather herbs directly from their natural habitat. If you are recording your own cultivations, you will still need most of these supplies. In your notebook, record the date, time, and location of where and when you took the specimen. Take a photo of the entire plant including the area in which it grows, if applicable. Depending on the time of year, you will want to include as much of the aerial parts of the plant that you can: leaves, stem, flowers, and fruit, depending on the season. Note that the appearance of herbs changes greatly as they progress through their life cycle. This is why recording the date and time is so important.

2. After cutting herbs with the snips or scissors, place them between 2 sheets of clean paper. Place the papers inside the heavy book. This will begin the drying and pressing process. Continue collecting until you have a good start on documenting your knowledge. If you are foraging, remember to wear gloves, especially if you are handling unknown plants. You should also bring a backpack to carry your supplies.

3. When you have a good start on your collection, it is time to start identifying, labeling, and properly drying and mounting your specimens. This can be done by keeping with some basic organizing principles and supplies. Some things you will need are:

   - Template to record your herb data
   - 2 wood blocks
   - 2 bricks
   - Clear contact paper

- Clear plastic sheet protectors
- Three-ring binder to store and organize your specimens and notes

4. Once you have returned home with your specimens, you will want to continue the drying process. Since the herbs have already been pressed at the time of gathering, you will want to handle them very carefully. Label a corner of the paper upon which they are drying with a sequential letter of the alphabet. Use this same letter to complete a data sheet template for each herb. It will include the following information:

- Type of herb
- Date, time, and location gathered
- Moon phase when gathered
- Physical description at time of gathering
- Uses and parts used

5. Recording this information and then coding each sheet with the same letter marked on the specimen will help you stay organized and make your herbarium more practical. Allow your herbs to dry completely by transferring them in between 2 wood blocks, such as two-by-fours, and then weighing down the blocks with bricks. Alternately, you can use a large and heavy book or a commercial flower press, which will come with paper to absorb moisture and heavy straps for pressing.

6. When the herbs are dry (this can take up to a week), carefully transfer them (including the drying paper if it has not stained or spoiled) onto the clear contact paper. Carefully and slowly press the clear contact paper over the herbs and gently smooth out bubbles. Trim off any excess contact paper. Slide the preserved herb specimen into one of the clear protective sheets and add it to the right-hand side of the binder. On the left-hand side, include another sheet protector with the data sheet inside. Using a three-ring binder allows you to organize your herbs however you wish. It can be done alphabetically or by type of use. Whichever method by which you choose to organize, having an herbarium for your coven or your personal use is one of the most significant grimoires a witch can create.

THE LIVING ALTAR

The altar is the setting upon which magickal work is created. An altar is both a hearth and a stage; a place to reflect and a place to take action. Using living herbs on your altar can strengthen your connection to the divine energies of the earth, the magick of the air, the importance of the sun, and the necessity of water. The living altar can be created inside or outside and can be made from a variety of materials. It can also be a small magickal potted garden that lives upon your altar. To create the living altar in a pot, you will need:

- Medium terra-cotta pot, 8 inches in diameter
- Black paint and a thin or narrow paintbrush
- Potting soil mixed with compost
- 1 (4-inch) plastic container for a potted herb such as thyme (healing), basil (happiness), mint (good luck), or sage (purity) with the simply stated intention for growth in one of those areas of spiritual development
- Green spell candle, around ¾-inch diameter and 6 inches tall
- Handful of colorful pebbles, tumbled stones, or crystals. You can choose these with intention and include a selection of carnelian, bloodstone, citrine, chalcedony, aventurine, and amethyst.
- Glass votive candle holder
- Joss stick of incense

1. Begin by turning the pot and feeling it. Measure four equidistant points on the outside of the pot and paint an elemental symbol at each point, in this order: earth, air, fire, and water going clockwise around the outside.

Earth   Air   Fire   Water

2. Fill the pot 3 inches from the top with the potting soil mix. Plant the herb close to the edge nearest the symbol for earth.
3. Opposite the herb, place the green candle directly in the potting soil and surround it with a few of the stones.

4. Take the glass votive holder and sink it into the soil next to the elemental water symbol, close to the edge of the pot with just the rim above the top of the soil. Press some more stones into the soil around the rim. Fill the votive holder with water.

5. Use some of the remaining stones to make a small mound beside the symbol for elemental air. Stick the joss stick in the middle of the stones, down into the soil so that it remains upright.

6. Place one of the crystals or any remaining stones in the center. The pot can live on your altar or on any sunny surface indoors or out, as it is a living altar in and of itself. When you use it for reflection, light the candle and the incense and meditate on your stated purpose that is aligned with your herb. Water the herb and make sure the votive container also has water. Blow across the water to see your breath ripple on the surface. Meditate for as long as the stick of incense burns, usually around half an hour. Reflect on the blessings of the spirit, the joy of practicing witchcraft, and the importance of spiritual growth. May your work be of benefit to all beings.

THE BROOM ON THE DOOR

Hanging a broom on the door is considered to be the witch's protection rite. Not only is the broom emblematic of witchcraft; it is associated with flying or astral projection as well as clearing and cleansing rituals both actual and symbolic. The broom on the door is a spell of protection on the home. The broom on the door is meant to keep out unwelcome guests. Creating your own herbal broom is a blessing upon your home, an emblem of your craft, and a method of bringing a powerful magickal tool into being. By using fresh herbs, you will also bring the earthy scent of combined herbs into your home. And by allowing your broom to dry naturally, you will have imbued your home with the energy and symbolism of the power of the broom and all it represents: freedom, flight, magick, wisdom, and power. You will need:

- Wood rasp or file
- Sturdy and smooth stick, preferably foraged, such as oak, linden, or hawthorn, 3–4 feet in length and approximately 1½ inches in diameter
- 100-grit sandpaper

- Selection of herbs with long stems such as sagebrush, mugwort, rosemary, and/or Scotch broom. Broom corn is traditionally used, and you may want to mix some in for structure and appearance.
- Jute twine
- Heavy scissors or garden shears
- Staple gun and staples
- 12-gauge copper wire
- Pliers
- Wire cutters

1. Prepare the broomstick by using the file or rasp to round off one end of the foraged stick. This will be the end that is not covered by herbs. Using a forward motion, smooth out any hard edges and give the end a soft appearance. Remove any bark from the shaft. Follow up with sandpaper to avoid splintering.

2. Gather your herbs into bundles with a little of each herb in each one. Try to make them all as equal in length as possible. Depending on the exact diameter of your broomstick, plan on preparing between eight and ten bundles and tying them together securely with the jute twine by tying a tight half knot, then flipping the bundle over and tying another half knot on the other side. Use the scissors or shears to cut the twine.

3. Position the bundles around the unfinished end of the broomstick about 4 inches from the end and staple them in place, alternating by stapling one bunch close to the top and the adjacent bunch close to the bottom until the broomstick is covered.

4. Take the pliers and bend the end of the copper wire at a 90-degree angle. The bent end of the wire should be the same length as the depth of one herb bunch. Insert the bent end of the wire in between two bunches of herbs very close to the top and very tightly wrap it around the herbs and the broomstick, securing all the elements together. Make at least three passes around the herb bundles and the broomstick, and more if you like, because the wire will make it very attractive. Using the wire cutters, snip the wire when you have made the desired amount of passes. With the pliers, bend the end of the wire and tuck it under the herbs so that it doesn't show.

5. Gather the herbs together just below the now-hidden end of the broomstick. You can tie them together tightly with the jute

twine, tie a double knot, and trim any excess twine. Then, cover the twine with another coil of copper wire. Your herbal broom is ready to impart its magick and protection to your surroundings! To boost its power, you can bless it with an incantation:

"STALK AND STEM
LEAF AND WOOD
USED FOR POWER
USED FOR GOOD
BY LIGHT OF DAY
OR DEAD OF NIGHT
UNWANTED ENERGIES
NOW TAKE FLIGHT
MY SACRED SPACE
IS NOW THIS ROOM
PROTECTED BY
MY MAGICK BROOM."

You can use the broom as part of a protection spell by preparing a chalice of water with three pinches of salt and three drops of sage oil. Dip the ends of the broom in the chalice and use it to asperge your surroundings; for example, the corners of your home or the boundaries of your property.

SACRED SAGE AND SMUDGING

In Native American culture, the practice of burning herbs such as sage is an ancient and sacred practice. It is done to bring about a balanced state of consciousness and is performed in a ritualistic manner. Generally referred to as "smudging," this English term is used to describe the ritual burning of sacred herbs in order to carry prayers, dispel negative energy, and prepare for greater rites. It is a spiritual expression, and indigenous people had their own words for smudging long before the practice was widely adopted and adapted by neopagans, new agers, and witches. Smudging became popular for three basic reasons: It is authentic, it is powerful, and it works. Common herbs used in smudging are sage, cedar, sweetgrass, and tobacco.

The smudging ceremony involves acknowledging the four directions, wafting the smoke from the burning herbs around a sacred space, around a person who will then also inhale the smoke. The smudging is done sometimes with a bundle of herbs tied together to form a "smudge stick." While honoring the indigenous and sacred origin of this herbal tradition—which, unless you are of Native American heritage is not your own to claim—you can still respectfully participate by creating your own smudge stick and using it appropriately in the context of a sacred ritual or in the preparation for one. The only necessary supplies are:

- Appropriate selection of herbs, such as sage (sage is the most common ingredient because it smolders after being lit and the flames are extinguished). Depending on your purpose, some other herbs you may want to add are:
  - Rosemary for its aroma and magickal properties, including creativity and invocation of memory as a way to honor your ancestors and relations
  - Lavender for healing and a sense of calm
  - Basil to make space for joy and to welcome prosperity
  - Mugwort to attune your psychic energy
  - Pine for purification
- Pair of scissors
- Thin cotton string

1. Gather your herbs together at the stem, making sure they are clean and dry and free from debris or unwanted plant material. It is not necessary to wash the herbs; in fact, it is best not to, as the excess moisture may cause them to rot. Use the scissors to trim the stems so that the herbs are about the same length, usually between 6 and 10 inches long and of sufficient volume to make a 1½-inch-diameter bundle. Tie the string very tightly around the base of the trimmed stems, leaving a "tail" of string that will be long enough to wrap around a few more times. Begin wrapping the long end of the string several times around the base of what will become the smudge stick.

2. On a slight diagonal, continue tightly wrapping the long end of the string around the herb bundle until you get to the top. Then, wrap the top by tightly winding the thread twice around and continuing to wrap back down the bundle on the opposite diagonal to create a crossing pattern. When you get to the bottom, tie the

The Modern Witchcraft Guide to Magickal Herbs

end of the string to the tail and finish with a strong knot. Allow the smudge stick to air-dry for about 2 weeks (less if it is a small stick). Use with respect, honor, and humility.

Afterword

Herbs are truly magickal and truly amazing. As we deepen our relationship with them, we come to understand all their power, beauty, mystery, and danger. Herbs have the power to cure and to kill. They can soothe and incite. They inspire wonder and madness. They grow, shift, transform, explore, and remind us always of our sacred connection to the earth and to each other. Herbs beckon us to gather over a cup of tea, to ponder our fortune and our fate. Herbs call us to the feast, enlivening the senses by engaging us with aroma and taste. Herbs impart their powers of seduction, sometimes making us believe that we can fly. Herbs are versatile. They can be beside us in the bath, as we rise into beauty and power, as we dare to give voice to our dearest hopes. We can ingest them, absorb them, claim a portion of their power for our own. They are our roots, the magickal beings that call us into nature with enticing fragrances, soft leaves, and beautiful blossoms. They soothe our spirits and make us contemplate the grand scheme of nature and our place in it. They instruct us how to be one with the earth; they are living proof that quiet strength and the ability to endure changing conditions are the keys to fruition. They encourage us to be at our best: healthy, radiant, and inspired.

Herbs inform our magickal practice. The more we learn about our sentient partners in magick, the more poignant our relationship becomes. We know that they respond to vibration, which is a type of hearing. We know that they are strong; their roots have the power to break apart concrete. We know that they can move, like the faces of the sunflowers follow the sun. They are possessed of a universal knowledge of harmony; they take what they need from their environment and ultimately return to it without needing to create the type of modifications that we humans seem to need in order to survive.

Herbs are the living embodiment of elemental magick. In herbs, we feel the culmination of seasons, the gentle rain that nourishes, and the roots that hold fast against fickle winds. We see the power of the sun, transformed into nutrients before our very eyes. We give thanks and honor herbs with joy.

Selected Bibliography

Aloi, Peg. "The Witch's Pharmacopoeia." *The Herb Quarterly*. Long Mountain Press. Fall 1999, p 49.

Brown, Diane. "A Brief History of Hops and Its Uses." www.canr.msu .edu/uploads/236/71516/ipm_academy_2014_intro_to_hops.pdf. Accessed 4/15/19.

Carr-Gomm, Philip, and Richard Heygate. *The Book of English Magic*. New York, Overlook Press, 2010, pp 97–100.

Chevalier, Gaétan, et al. "Earthing: Health Implications of Reconnecting the Human Body to the Earth's Surface Electrons." *Journal of Environmental and Public Health*. 291541, 2012, www.ncbi .nlm.nih.gov/pmc/articles/PMC3265077/. Accessed 2/27/2019.

"Composting at Home." *EPA*. www.epa.gov/recycle/ composting-home. Accessed 3/25/19.

"Croton lechleri." Memorial Sloan Kettering Cancer Center. www.mskcc.org/cancer-care/integrative-medicine/herbs/ croton-lechleri. Accessed 5/30/19.

Culpeper, Nicholas. *Complete Herbal*. Forgotten Books, 2016.

Day, Alice. "A Witch's Garden." *The Herb Quarterly*. Long Mountain Press. Fall 1999, p 51.

Elhakeem, Ali, et al. "Aboveground Mechanical Stimuli Affect Belowground Plant-Plant Communication." *PLOS One* (13)5, 2018. https://doi.org/10.1371/journal.pone.0195646. Accessed 2/26/19.

Faragher, Aliza Kelly. "Your Essential Guide to Tasseography, the Practice of Reading Tea Leaves." *Allure*, May 7, 2018. www.allure .com/story/how-to-read-tea-leaves-tasseography.

Hansen, Harold A. *The Witch's Garden*. Santa Cruz, Unity Press, 1978.

Hyatt, Richard. *Chinese Herbal Medicine: Ancient Art and Modern Science*. New York, Schocken Books, 1978.

Kotta, Sabhna, Shahid H. Ansari, and Javed Ali. "Exploring Scientifically Proven Aphrodisiacs." *Pharmacognosy Review* 7(13) 2013. www.ncbi.nlm.nih.gov/pmc/articles/PMC3731873/. Accessed 2/27/19.

Pettitt, Edward Thomas. *A Critical Edition of the Old English 'Lacnunga.'* King's College, London, 1996.

Rätsch, Christian. *Plants of Love: Aphrodisiacs in History and a Guide to Their Identification*. Berkeley, Ten Speed Press, 1997.

Sossamon, Jeff. "Plants Respond to Leaf Vibrations Caused by Insects' Chewing, MU Study Finds." *University of Missouri News Bureau*. https://munews.missouri.edu/news-releases/2014/0701-plants-respond-to-leaf-vibrations-caused-by-insects%E2%80%99-chewing-mu-study-finds/. Accessed 2/26/19.

Streisand, Opal. *Sacred Herbs*. London, Quarto Publishing, 2017.

Strgar, Wendy. *Sex That Works: An Intimate Guide to Awakening Your Erotic Life*. Boulder, Sounds True, 2017.

Tyler, Varro E. *The Honest Herbal: A Sensible Guide to the Use of Herbs and Related Remedies*. New York, Pharmaceutical Products Press, 1993.

Wagner Engel, Caroline. *The Greek God of Healing Asclepius & Goddess of Health Hygeia: A Double-Gendered Double-Deity Model*. Diss. Yale University, 2009, https://elischolar.library.yale.edu/ymtdl/61/. Accessed 3/31/19.

INDEX